The Silent Spring of Rachel Carson

Paul Lobo Portugés

Plain View Press
P. O. 42255
Austin, TX 78704

plainviewpress.net
sb@plainviewpress.net
1-512-441-2452

Copyright Paul Lobo Portugés, 2009. All rights reserved.
ISBN: 978-0-9819731-0-4
Library of Congress Number: 2009926074

Cover design by Susan Bright

Introduction

I first read Rachel Carson's *Silent Spring* when I was in college. Her startling book had little to do with the struggle Ms. Carson went through while writing her infamous study of the chemical poisoning of America. Naturally, I had no idea that the story behind the story was inspirational and important. Years later, while I was working on a screenplay about religious persecution in Iran, I came across a PBS documentary on Rachel Carson. I mentioned the story to a producer I was working for. He said it sounded interesting. His wife said it was a wonderful story, that we should make a film about her.

After finishing my work on *Behind the Veil* in Australia, I took a side trip on my way back to the States and visited the Beinecke Library at Yale University. I spent a week or so reading stacks of Ms. Carson's journals, letters, papers. A young graduate student was also turning Ms. Carson's pages. She was a research assistant for a professor who was writing a new biography of Rachel Carson.

I went back to Hollywood and pitched the story about Ms. Carson's struggle to write and publish *Silent Spring*. My agent and I toured the usual suspects: Universal, Fox, etc. A successful action director was interested. He had optioned my Shakespeare script (*Shakespeare's Second Best Bed*) the year before. My agent nixed optioning the "Carson project," as he called it, demanding that one option/development deal was enough. We finally took an offer from an independent producer who swore Carson's story was "important, a sure thing." I struggled with the "Carson project" on and off for the next year. At the same time, I was in Europe writing another "environmental project," *The Man Who Planted Trees*. Since *Trees* was on the "fast track," I didn't complete the first draft of *Silent Spring* until some time the following spring. Unfortunately, by that time, the producer who had optioned it was in pre-production on an "important" historical drama, and he lost interest in the "Carson project."

Though disappointed, I wasn't surprised; my agent was determined to find someone else to buy the script. He sent it around to several independent companies. Meanwhile, I began work on adapting a newly discovered manuscript of Robert Lewis Stevenson's short story,

"The Enchantress," for another producer, unfortunately a chain smoker, making it difficult for me to work with him. To compromise, we would meet in "the great outdoors," as he liked to call the Santa Anita racetrack. Like his father, he liked to "tinker" (his phrase) with his writer's scripts. Consequently, the work on "The Enchantress" took much longer than I had expected. Meanwhile, my agent had found an independent production company that was interested in the "Carson project"– on the condition I would re-write and have the final draft ready in two months. Unfortunately, I couldn't get away from the clouds of smoke at the race track, so I had to back out of the "low budget, artsy Carson deal," as my agent now called it.

Some months after I finally completed my work on the Stevenson story, I got a call: "You remember that story about the little, old lady from, where was it..." "Maine," I replied, "little, old Rachel Carson, *Silent Spring*..." "Yeah, yeah, that's the one." His wife had been after him to pursue the idea. I met with him (and his wife) and one of my favorite directors to discuss the script. The producer's wife convinced all of us that the script, with a little more work, was a star vehicle for the usual core of "older A-list" actresses (Meryl Steep, Susan Sarandon) who would do it for next to nothing. They made some calls and tried to raise development money. His wife suggested they sell one of their Picassos and get started right away.

Later that month, the director called and asked if I'd like to have coffee. He introduced me to his partners in film. They had bought the rights to an autobiographical book about the revolutionary struggle in Nicaragua, *Fire From the Mountain*. Would I be interested? "What about "little, old Rachel Carson?" I suggested. "First Nicaragua, then *Silent Spring*." My agent said "deal," and once again I worked on another project, rather than the one closest to my heart. In fact, I worked an additional project for the same director, a documentary about the Mafia in Sicily while I was writing *Fire*. And to make the Rachel Carson producer happy, I did a polish for him on a film he was about to shoot in Africa. And after that, I sold my script about racism and a Cuban family in Florida during the Cuban Missile Crisis, and after that I adapted Melville's novel about incest, bohemians, and the upper class – *Pierre*.

Obviously, *The Silent Spring of Rachel Carson* had yet to be made. Even after I was awarded the "Focus Best Independent Screenplay" award, I could not quite convince other producers to make my favorite project. The script has been optioned since then, but a similar project at HBO (never made) cooled the interest in my competing "little, old Rachel Carson" story. My agent, God bless him, suggested finding someone to publish the script: "...people'll read it, get really excited, and buy the rights, and make a movie starring..." Who knows?

Note:
The Silent Spring of Rachel Carson is "inspired" by my research at the Yale Beinecke Library. It is not intended to be a factual recreation of Rachel Carson's struggle to write and publish *Silent Spring*. Most of the characters, names, many of the events in my screenplay have been changed and/or fictionalized in order to create a dramatic story.

THE SILENT SPRING OF RACHEL CARSON

BLACK SCREEN:

TITLE: Inspired by a true story.

FADE IN:

EXT. SKY VIEW OF A SMALL TOWN IN FARM COUNTRY - DAY

An AMERICAN BALD EAGLE's POV as it flies over checkerboard fields near a small farm town: grainfields, orchards, wildflower pastures. Cows graze, BIRDS SING LOUDLY.

> RACHEL CARSON (V.O.)
> White clouds drift above.

The EAGLE'S POV: Oak, maple, birch against a background of mist-covered pine woods. Foxes barking; deer cross a pasture into the woods. The EAGLE SWOOPS down over plum trees and kills a MOUSE in its talons, lands. The EAGLE'S POV: rushing brooks, frogs croaking, etc.

> RACHEL (V.O.)
> Foxes bark in the hills and deer silently
> walk into the pine woods, hidden in an
> early morning mist.

RACHEL CARSON, 6, in her Sunday best, riding on the shoulders of her FATHER, 37, baggy pants, bow tie. She tries to catch falling PLUM BLOSSOMS; she is so excited she almost falls off her father's shoulders.

> FATHER
> Careful Rachel.

A SHADOW passes over the SUN. They see something: her Father puts her down. They run away from a BILLOWY CLOUD (DDT) gently raining down, obscuring them, the trees, the deer.

The EAGLE abandons its kill and takes off, flying through the DDT cloud. The Eagle's POV: the deer fall down, dying, the foxes stop barking, lay down, DYING.

BIRDS' SONG DECREASES; a SPARROW falls to the ground, gasps for air.

The DDT CLOUD ENVELOPS Rachel and her Father. Rachel screams, but we HEAR NOTHING as they become INVISIBLE.

NO SOUND.

The LANDSCAPE TRANSFORMS: plants wither, trees TRANSFORM into leafless skeletons.

The SPARROW'S BODY TRANSFORMS TO BONE, TO DUST.

The SCREEN turns SUNLIGHT-WHITE, THEN BLACK.

FADE IN:

EXT. RACHEL CARSON'S COTTAGE NEAR WEST SOUTHPORT, MAINE – FIRST LIGHT SKY – 1960

The rugged Maine shoreline near the mouth of the Shepscot River. Rachel Carson's board'n'batten cottage (with screened porch), surrounded by pine, spruce, birch.

O.S. RACHEL'S SCREAM.

Frightened BIRDS FLY OFF.

INT. RACHEL CARSON'S COTTAGE - SAME
RACHEL'S BEDROOM.

Windows all around, no curtains. In bed, RACHEL CARSON, late 40's, frail, startles herself awake. LOUISE GOODWOMAN, 39 - lithe, sophisticated, a manuscript of poems on her chest - is half-asleep on the bedroom divan.

>   LOUISE
>   Rachel?
>
>   RACHEL
>   Sorry, Louise, bad dream.

Rachel puts on her terrycloth bathrobe.

>   LOUISE
>   You okay?
>
>   RACHEL
>   Thank you, yes, just a dream, really.
>
>   LOUISE
>   Write it down and forget it.

Rachel exits into the HALLWAY, then into

MARIA CARSON'S BEDROOM.

MARIA CARSON, 70ish, flinty, stares out the window at the dawn sky. Rachel kisses her.

>   MARIA
>   Just look at that sky - makes me want to
>   give up painting.

RACHEL
Sleep well mamma?

Maria uncovers Rebecca, 6, hiding in her bed under the blankets.

MARIA
Not with little Miss Wiggly sneaking in
in the middle of the night.

RACHEL
Rebecca, not again!

REBECCA
Sorry, Auntie Rachel.

MARIA
Sorry? Sorry is for sorry people.

Rachel exits into her

SCREENED PORCH. A FEW MINUTES LATER.

The porch in the early morning misty light.

Rachel sits at her desk, types on her Royal typewriter.

JEFFIE, her calico cat, waits for a caress. Rachel smiles at Jeffie, pets her.

Louise enters, kisses Rachel on the head while Rachel continues writing.

RACHEL
Dream, dream, go away. I'm writing it
down like you said.

>   LOUISE
> My place, five minutes, okay? Hurry!

Rachel nods. Louise exits. Rachel types a little, then puts on her coat, exits.

EXT. RACHEL'S COTTAGE - DAWN

Rachel gets in her WOODY station wagon. Jeffie hops on the hood. Rachel smiles, open the door, Jeffie gets in. Rachel drives off.

In her wicker wheelchair, Maria enters the screened porch:

>   MARIA
> Don't be too long, darling. We have to
> pack.

Maria watches the sky, aglow, just before sunrise; Rebecca enters, holds her hand as they watch the sky turn colors.

>   MARIA (CONT'D)
>   (to Rebecca)
> God bless God.

EXT. MARY'S COTTAGE/BIRD SANCTUARY OVERLOOKING THE SEA - SUNRISE

Rachel pulls up, her POV: Louise, sitting in front of her cottage near a bed of HYACINTHS, listening to BIRDS singing.

The sun rises over the ocean. Delighted, Rachel sits next to Louise, puts her arm around her. Jeffie jumps into her lap. Rachel laughs joyfully. Louise too.

                    RACHEL
          Paradise.

INT. MOVING CAR – NIGHT

Rachel, Jeffie, and Louise in front, Rebecca and Maria in back.

                    LOUISE
          I promised Sam I'd be back in Boston by–

                    RACHEL
          – Sam, of course.

                    LOUISE
          He is my husband–

                    RACHEL
          – And you're the dutiful wife.

                    LOUISE
          At least we've managed a week together. You, me, your mother, your niece, and your writing.

                    RACHEL
          You're a poet, surely you understand.

They pass a DRIVE-IN movie, MOVIE-TONE NEWS on the screen featuring J.F.K.'s election campaign.

                    REBECCA
          Look!

Their POV: MOVIE-TONE NEWS: J.F.K. in a Boston PARADE. We stay on the MOVIE-TONE NEWS, as Rachel's WOODY passes on: MOVIETONE NEWSREEL MONTAGE:

A. INT. AUDITORIUM- NEW YORK - DAY

Rachel receives a National Council of Women's Book Award from the N.C.W. CHAIRWOMAN. The Audience's standing ovation embarrasses Rachel.

> MOVIETONE NARRATOR (V.O.)
> Rachel Carson, America's famous naturalist, continuing in the tradition of Henry David Thoreau and John Muir, received one of the nation's highest honors–

> CHAIRWOMAN
> (to the Crowd)
> – Thank you, thank you. Miss Carson has kindly agreed to answer a few questions.

> WOMAN
> What are you writing now Miss Carson?

> RACHEL
> A children's book, about nature– *A Sense of Wonder* perhaps– I'm still not sure about the title.

> BEATNIK WOMAN
> What about nuclear pollution?

> WOMAN #2
> Will you please write another book about the sea?

B. EXT. MAINE SEASHORE - DAY

Rachel, Rebecca and SEVERAL CHILDREN examine an OCTOPUS in a tidepool.

>   MOVIETONE NARRATOR (V.O.)
>   Seashore to seashore, Miss Carson's
>   passion for the natural world is
>   appreciated by young-

C. EXT. SAN FRANCISCO SEASHORE - DAY

The Golden Gate Bridge in the b.g., Rachel - surrounded by several middle-age BIRD WATCHERS - sights a GREY BLUE HERON taking off.

>   MOVIETONE NARRATOR (V.O.)
>   - and old.

D. EXT. SEASHORE - DAY

Under cover of a canopy during a rainstorm, Rachel types while the sea rages in the b.g.

>   MOVIETONE NARRATOR (V.O.)
>   When America's Grandame of Nature is
>   not busy at her typewriter-

E. EXT. MUIR WOODS, CALIFORNIA - DAY

Surrounded by scores of CHILDREN on a ridge top, each holding a tree seedling. Rachel dedicates a Redwood Grove, while planting a seedling.

>   MOVIETONE NARRATOR (V.O.) (cont'd)
>   - often she is championing the
>   beleaguered environment. God bless Mother
>   Nature and God bless Miss Rachel Carson
>   for her writings about the wonders of
>   nature.

END MOVIETONE NEWSREEL MONTAGE

INT. MOVING TRAIN - RACHEL'S COMPARTMENT- NIGHT

Rachel, in her upper bunk, looks through photographs of CLOUDS, while typing.

Rebecca, wearing a Yankee's baseball cap, sleeps below; the door to the ajoining compartment is open: Maria sleeps in lower bunk. Louise combs her hair. Rachel hands her photos.

>   RACHEL
>   (referring to the photographs)
> Extraordinary!

>   LOUISE
> My Sam is a gifted photographer.

They look at a photo of cumulus clouds.

INT. CBS OMNIBUS STUDIOS - DAY

On SEVERAL MONITORS: pictures of white CLOUDS, then STORM CLOUDS. Rachel, wearing headphones, narrates from her manuscript while the sound tech- DAVE, black horned rimmed glasses- records under the direction of VINCENT FRASER- a dapper English bloke.

Rebecca, pounding her baseball glove trying to garner attention, irritates Vincent. He shushes her.

>   RACHEL (V.O.)
> Some of our fondest memories are the images of clouds drifting by overhead- or sometimes the sad memory of storm clouds bringing rain, snow, or- on occasion- disaster.

Rebecca becomes alarmed by pictures on the monitor of natural disasters.

          REBECCA
Auntie!

          VINCENT
Shhh!

          RACHEL (V.O.)
Without the miracle of clouds and rain,
the continents would have remained barren
and uninhabited, and perhaps life would
never have evolved beyond the fishes.

At this point, Rebecca makes a "fish-face" at Vincent.

          VINCENT
Cut! Excellent, Rachel. Would you mind
if the child waited outside!

          RACHEL
Yes, I would mind. Rebecca!

          REBECCA
Sorry. When can we see my mamma?

          RACHEL
Sorry is only a word.

Enter BILL LAKES – 45, natty, sophisticated, Rachel's editor – with a letter in his hand.

BILL
Hello Rachel.
   (to Rebecca)
Hello little one- the Yankees going to win the pennant this year? Huh?
   (no response from Rebecca)
As your editor, I am happy to report our dear publisher has approved your proposal for the sea anthology-

RACHEL
Wonderful.

BILL
However-
   (reading the letter)
- "we still look forward to your children's book (as yet still untitled) which is now several-

RACHEL & BILL
- "months behind schedule."

REBECCA
Auntie, please-

RACHEL
Rebecca, we're talking.

BILL
Shawn at *The New Yorker* magazine is interested in your idea about the planet as a living organism-

VINCENT
Ready Miss Carson! Dave, bring up the puffy ones.

Dave signals Rachel to begin. We SEE various shots of cumulus clouds. Dave brings up the sound, LOUDER & LOUDER. The clouds turn to STORM CLOUDS, LIGHTNING AND THUNDER.

Rebecca hides her eyes. Bill comforts her:

> RACHEL (V.O.)
> As the earth warms under the morning sun, invisible columns of warm air begin to rise- from a plowed field, a lake, a town. The rising air cools at a certain point. It can no longer contain its water invisibly, and the white misty substance of a cloud is born. Cumulus clouds can be an aviator's promise of good flying weather, or an omen of furious turbulence hidden within their calm exterior.

> VINCENT
> Cut. That's a print, Dave.
> (to Rebecca)
> Surely you're not afraid of a little lightning and thunder, are you young lady?

Rebecca runs outside, Rachel follows.

EXT. CBS STUDIOS - STORMY DAY

Rain, lightning, and thunder. Rachel finds Rebecca sulking in a corner. Bill flags down a taxi.

> RACHEL
> I'm sorry you had to wait so long. Let's go get that surprise for your mamma, okay?

Taxi stops. Bill gets in. Rachel holds out her hand to
Rebecca. She doesn't respond, still cowering in the corner.

    TAXI DRIVER
  For crying out loud, lady! I ain't got
  all day.

    BILL
  Relax, why don't you?

Rachel takes off her rain hat, steps away from the building,
and puts her face up so the rain splashes her. She twirls.

    TAXI DRIVER
  She nuts?

Rachel holds her hand out for Rebecca. Lightning! She waits
for her, Rebecca finally takes her hand. They dance in the rain.

    BILL
  Crazier than a bedbug.

INT. DEPARTMENT STORE – DOWNTOWN BOSTON – DAY

Scores of T.V.'S tuned to the NIXON-J.F.K debate while Rachel
and Rebecca (still dripping from the rain) and Bill wait in a
record booth. A SALESMAN nods to Rachel, and the booth fills
with BEETHOVEN'S VIOLIN CONCERTO.

    BILL
  Reader's Digest wants to do a few
  excerpts from your sea anthology,
  providing you write a short lead-in–

While Bill goes on and on, Rachel holds Rebecca's hand and
"dissolves" into Beethoven.

INT. HOSPITAL - NIGHT

In the hall, Rachel confers with a DOCTOR. Discouraged, she thanks him, and enters Marjorie's room. Maria and Marjorie listen to Beethoven. MARJORIE, 27, Rachel's niece (Rebecca's mother), gaunt and sickly, motions for Rachel to come sit near her. In a corner, Rebecca finishes her drawing of her and Marjorie floating in a cloudless sky. She shows the picture to Marjorie.

>MARJORIE
That's beautiful Rebecca. Oh Aunt Rachel, thank you.

>RACHEL
Don't thank me, thank Beethoven. The Doctor says that soon you can come stay with us, until you get your strength back.

>MARJORIE
Please, if something should happen to me-

>MARIA
- Nonsense, Marjorie, you're a Carson.

INT. PARK - DAY

Rachel's POV: migrating Canadian geese overhead. Rebecca sails her boat on the park lake.

>MARIA
But Rebecca is family.

>RACHEL
I've hardly the time or energy to become a full time mother. Between my work and-

MARIA
– taking care of me. Marjorie will get better, she always has.

INT. MOVING CAR – NIGHT

Rachel and Maria up front, Rebecca and Marjorie in back.

RACHEL
Bill likes the idea for my new book, I think.

MARIA
Which one? You haven't finished the two you're working on now!

RACHEL
You want to hear what I've in mind?

MARJORIE
I would.

REBECCA
Is it about me?

RACHEL
About all of us. If we, humans, plan to survive this new atomic age, we must do so with humility, not arrogance.

MARIA
Please Rachel, don't preach. And first things first, finish what you've already started.

EXT. OCEAN - WOODEN DIVING BOAT - DAY

CAPTAIN BILL - salt of the earth, pipe smoker - charts the boat's location. Rebecca, wearing a yellow rain coat, looks at the bubbles from the diver beneath the sea. The diver's air compressor starts sputtering.

> CAPTAIN BILL
> Do me a favor mate, give that thing a
> good kick, will you?

The compressor backfires. Rebecca timidly edges toward it.

> CAPTAIN BILL (cont'd)
> Mind you don't hit it too hard, or it may
> well explode. Lost my second mate that
> way off the China coast not too long ago.

Rebecca is scared. Bill mimes how to kick it. Rebecca kicks it, and it runs smoothly again. She is proud of herself.

EXT. UNDER THE SEA - DAY

Rachel, in an old fashion diving suit, PHOTOGRAPHS a school of jelly fish. Above her, a couple of sharks swim back and forth, which catches Rachel's attention; then she sees thousands of dead fish floating on the surface.

EXT. BOAT - DAY

Captain Bill helps Rachel pull off her diving helmet. The first thing she sees is Rebecca, smacking (with a pole) at the thousands of dead fish surrounding the boat. Rachel demands the pole.

                    RACHEL
          No.

She takes the pole away.

                    CAPTAIN BILL
          Happens about every time those damn
          government planes spray near the river.

                    RACHEL
          Have you reported –

A Fish and Wildlife boat approaches.

                    CAPTAIN BILL
          – Hell, the sheriff just laughed.

Rachel scoops up a fish, inspects it. ELIOT STANFORD, 48, slender, pulls up in the FISH AND WILDLIFE boat.

                    ELIOT
          I wouldn't eat that if I were you.

                    RACHEL
          Eliot. Eliot Stanford!

                    ELIOT
          Why, if it isn't "Miss Right and Bright."
          I didn't recognize you in your new
          outfit.

EXT. SHORE - DAY

Rachel and Rebecca inside, Eliot leans against Rachel's car.

                ELIOT
Would I kid a good looking gal like
you - enough DDT to kill a small town of
God-fearing, hard working Americans.

                RACHEL
I'll believe it when I see the official
analysis. In the meantime, why not stop
it, the spraying, as a precaution?

                ELIOT
"It"? "It" the Chemical Boys or "It" the
U.S. of A.?

                REBECCA
I'm hungry.

                RACHEL
Come by before you go back to D.C. - talk
over old times.

                ELIOT
Nothing's changed: the environment's
going to hell faster than -

                REBECCA
Auntie!

                ELIOT
I'll call you.

                RACHEL
That's what you said years ago.

INT./EXT. CARSON COTTAGE – NIGHT

SCREEN PORCH:

Rachel types. She hears the WIND, listens, stops typing. She coughs, feels a pain in her chest. She walks

OUTSIDE:

She massages the pain in her chest, breathes her pain away as she listens to the night sounds. Maria enters the PORCH:

> MARIA
> You still working?

> RACHEL
> Oh! You startled me.

> MARIA
> I'm sorry I'm such a burden to you.

> RACHEL
> Mamma!

The PHONE RINGS.

> RACHEL
> I'll get it.

Rachel enters the house, answers the phone in the

FRONT ROOM:

Maria enters, lights a candle in front of a PHOTOGRAPH of Rachel, 6, picking plumb blossoms with her Father, (reminiscent of her dream).

                    RACHEL (cont'd)
          Hello...Louise?...Me too...I found a
          local girl to tidy your cottage...
          Thursday...How wonderful. Marjorie will
          be home from the hospital. Sam coming?

EXT. SEASHORE - DAY

Marjorie, Rachel, and Maria picnic. Rachel writes in her notebook. Marjorie reads from the Song of Solomon. Rebecca chases SEAGULLS near the surf.

                    MARJORIE
          From the Song of Solomon: "for lo winter
          is past, the rain is over and gone. The
          flowers appear on the earth."

Rebecca almost gets knocked down by a wave.

                    MARIA
          Rebecca! Be careful. Rachel.

Maria motions for Rachel to go after Rebecca. She does.

                    MARJORIE
          "The time of the singing of birds is come
          and the voice of the earth is heard
          throughout our land."

NEAR THE SURF:

Waves pound the shore as Rebecca and Rachel walk along the ragged coast looking at tidepools.

                    RACHEL
          Your mother and I used to walk along
          here.

> REBECCA
> You and your mom too?

Rachel nods yes.

> REBECCA (cont'd)
> And her mother and hers? Did you know my dad before he –

> RACHEL
> (reluctant)
> – Yes, I knew him. Look – a sea anemone.

She touches the anemone. A little wary, Rebecca touches it. A wave CRASHES; they run back, laughing. In the b.g.: Louise and her husband, SAM GOODMAN, 35, goatee, run toward Rachel. Sam carries two dead black-throated green warblers.

> LOUISE
> Rachel! They've killed everything!

The waves drown out Rachel's voice as she calms Louise.

EXT. LOUISE AND SAM'S COTTAGE/BIRD SANCTUARY – DAY

Near their cottage at the edge of a lagoon, Rachel, Louise, and Sam are long-faced: hundreds of dead birds, dead fish, dying butterflies, etc. Louise soothes a dying SWAN.

Rachel's POV: a BUTTERFLY lands on the car hood. It struggles to fly. One wing moves, ever so slowly. She picks it up. The wind comes up; a DEAD BUTTERFLY drifts down, then another, then scores of dead butterflies fall.

All the while, a low roar gets louder: BIPLANES.

SAM
Bastards!

They hurry to Rachel's car. BIPLANES make their approach, turn on the DDT GAS CLOUDS.

Sam, Rachel, and Louise get in the car. Sam tries to start the car, no luck. Sam gets out, looks under the hood. Rachel gets out to help Sam.

SAM (cont'd)
Get back in the car.

RACHEL
The coil wire.

LOUISE
Rachel!

Rachel attaches the coil wire.

SAM
Try it now.

Louise tries to start the car – no luck. Rachel fidgets with the wire.

SAM (cont'd)
I'll get an injunction.

RACHEL
She's flooding it. You try Sam.

The BIPLANES are very close. Sam gets in the car, starts it! Rachel tries to wave off the Biplanes.

                    RACHEL (cont'd)
                Stop! You fools! Stop!

The PILOT ROCKS HIS WINGS, thinking Rachel is waving "Hello,"
then flies over Rachel, enveloping her and the car in a dense
cloud of DDT. Coughing, Rachel gets in the car.

INT. MOVING CAR - SAME

                    LOUISE
                Where the hell do they think this is—
                Nazi Germany?

The cloud is so thick, Sam almost drives off the road into
the estuary. Louise screams. He backs up, and slowly they
emerge from the DDT cloud. The Biplanes fly away.

                    LOUISE (cont'd)
                Smells like kerosene.

                    RACHEL
                    (angry, coughing)
                What? Right.

                    SAM
                God damn idiots!

Louise soothes Rachel as they drive along the river, the sun
sets blood red on the horizon. Rachel reaches into her coat
pocket, opens her hands: the monarch BUTTERFLY.

E.C.U.: THE BUTTERFLY OPENS AND CLOSES ITS WINGS,
SLOWLY.

INT. RACHEL'S COTTAGE - NIGHT

RACHEL'S KITCHEN:

Louise washes Rachel's hair. A tea pot begins to whistle.
They make tea, occasionally overhearing Maria and Sam arguing in the front room.

>LOUISE
>I suppose it's the gypsy moths or us.

>RACHEL
>That's what they want us to "suppose."
>How's your book?

>LOUISE
>A lot of half written poems laughing at me. You know the feeling- no, I take it back. The muse adores you.

>RACHEL
>Don't I wish. It's a miracle I get anything done these days.

>LOUISE
>Maria and Rebecca are one thing, but I could never deal with your niece, Marjorie. That didn't come out the way I meant. It's just ever since I was a little girl, my mother's cancer, she suffered so long. I know it's irrational, but sickness, the pain, I couldn't do what you do, I just couldn't.

> RACHEL
> Marjorie is the real heroine, she tries
> so hard not to be a bother.

Louise hugs Rachel. With the tea, they enter the

FRONT ROOM:

> SAM
> The legal question is –

> MARIA
> You a photographer or a lawyer?

> SAM
> Do the Feds have the right to poison us
> without our consent?

> LOUISE
> That's a bit cynical.

> SAM
> The chemical companies'll do whatever
> they want, unless someone stops them.

> MARIA
> And that's you and Louise, the
> photographer and the poet?

> SAM
> And why not?

> MARIA
> Any idiot knows you can't sue Uncle Sam
> and win! Louise, put yourself to good
> use, won't you dear, and see if Marjorie
> would like some tea.

LOUISE
Oh, I thought she was asleep.

RACHEL
I'll go.

While Louise pours tea, Rachel walks toward Marjorie's bedroom.

SAM
So I'm an idiot, but I'm–

LOUISE
– but you're right. Count me in, dear husband.

MARIA
You're not serious!

SAM
Thank you dear wife. A family that sues together, stays together. What do you say, Rachel?

Rachel's POV: Rebecca and MARJORIE praying in their room.

RACHEL
I'd like to, but–

SAM
– Two women are better than one.

LOUISE
Bravo Sam.
(to Rachel)
It would give us more time together.

Sam gets their coats as they head for the door.

> RACHEL
> Courtrooms, lawyers, no thanks.

> MARIA
> (to Sam and Louise)
> Why not join the Red Cross instead!

> SAM
> (to Rachel)
> I'll do the paperwork, you do the research.

Rachel helps Louise on with her coat.

> RACHEL
> I'm a nature writer, Sam, not a rabble rouser.

EXT. RACHEL CARSON'S COTTAGE – STARRY, STARRY NIGHT

Maria waits on the porch while Sam, Louise, and Rachel walk to Sam's car. The sky is overwhelming: a blanket of stars.

> SAM
> (looking up at the stars)
> There are things in the heavens, Maria.

> LOUISE
> There is a God!

> MARIA
> (pointing to the night sky)
> This is what you are meant to write about.

                    RACHEL
              Good night you two.

                    LOUISE
              Good night darling.

INT./EXT. RACHEL'S COTTAGE – EARLY MORNING

BEDROOM: Rachel writes in her journal. She hears a car.

Eliot drives up in Fish and Wildlife truck. He gets out, admires Rachel's cottage, honks the horn, Rachel exits.

                    RACHEL
              Careful or you'll raise the dead!

                    ELIOT
                (referring to the cottage)
              You must have sold a hell of a lot of
              coffee table books to afford this beauty.

                    RACHEL
              Tens of thousands, thank you.

He hands her SCIENTIFIC PAPERS.

                    ELIOT
              Here, a little homework for you.

                    RACHEL
              Why Eliot, you shouldn't have.

ELIOT
It's the report on those dead fish that
so rudely interrupted your pretty
picture taking the other day – Enough DDT
to wipe out half a Soviet army battalion.

RACHEL
Don't they realize what they're
doing?

ELIOT
Sure they do: making millions, hand over
foot. That's why I thought you'd like to
help.

RACHEL
You're the government, just stop.

ELIOT
Stop progress? Greed – it's the American
way.

RACHEL
Still bitter after all these years.

ELIOT
You would be too if you'd spent the last
five years fighting these sons of
bitches.

RACHEL
You'll get to them.

ELIOT
Not without some help. How's about you
get dressed and we take a little ride?

                    RACHEL
            Where to?

                    ELIOT
            To hell and – hopefully – back.

EXT. COUNTRY – SUNSET

They drive along a road lined with laurels and alders.

                    RACHEL (V.O.)
                (while writing in her
                notebook)
            Laurels and alder. Sparrows –

Sparrows feed on berries and peck at weed pods.

                    RACHEL (V.O.) (cont'd)
            – feeding on the seed heads of dried
            weeds rising–

Eliot plays "chicken" with a DETOUR sign.

                    ELIOT
                (mumbling)
            Detour, my ass–

                    RACHEL
                (referring to the sign)
            – Eliot!

Eliot goes around the sign.

                    ELIOT
            They make believe they're not poisoning
            us, I can make believe their sign wasn't
            there.

He drives on. WORKERS flag him to stop, but he ignores them.

Rachel's POV: fields dotted with white powder (dieldrin) splotches. They pass several government SEMI-TRUCKS. WORKERS in SPACE SUIT PROTECTIVE GEAR drag the carcasses of dead sheep. Other WORKERS throw dead sheep into one of the semi-trucks. A SPACE SUIT WORKER stops them.

> WORKER
> Go back and take the detour.

Eliot turns back, but takes pictures first.

> ELIOT
> Some idiot forgot to read the directions
> on the dieldrin bags.

EXT. TYPICAL AMERICAN MIDDLE CLASS NEIGHBORHOOD – DAY

Rachel and Eliot parked on a sidestreet. They wait.

> ELIOT
> The boys're a little behind schedule.

> RACHEL
> You expect me to believe the government
> is, knowingly, spraying the entire
> population with poison.

> ELIOT
> Worse than that: they're now gearing up
> to spray every acre of the good ole U.S.
> of A., to make sure we rid America of all
> our "icky" insects, sea to shining sea.

                    RACHEL
          Really, Eliot, don't be absurd.

A DDT TRUCK MAKING A DDT SPRAY RUN appears down the
tree-lined street. Eliot backs the car up and speeds away to
avoid being sprayed while Rachel watches in horror as PEOPLE
are enveloped in the billowy, pure white DDT clouds.

                    ELIOT
          They've got to do to it, to save the world
          for democracy.

                    RACHEL
          What are you talking about?

                    ELIOT
          Apparently, you haven't heard about the
          red ant – a Communist plot to overthrow
          the government.

She laughs.

                    ELIOT (cont'd)
          I'm not kidding.

He hands her a brochure with a cartoonish Red Ant portrayed
as a Communist Spy (hammer and sickle, Soviet flag, etc.)

EXT. SWIMMING POOL – DAY

As they pull up to the swimming pool parking lot:

                    ELIOT
          My latest research shows that DDT is
          several times more toxic to children.

DDT TRUCKS spray excited CHILDREN rollicking in the toxic
clouds.

RACHEL
It's madness!

ELIOT
But they're saving us from polio, the dreaded gypsy moth- people like me.

RACHEL
Why are you showing me this?

ELIOT
Because I need your help.

RACHEL
What could I possibly do?

ELIOT
Write! Write about it.

RACHEL
You too, huh. I'm already two books behind schedule, my mother's 86 years old, Marjorie-

ELIOT
- Twenty five years from now, half the population of this country will mysteriously develop cancer.

INT./EXT. RACHEL'S COTTAGE - FULL MOON NIGHT

Rachel is at her desk on the PORCH. She reads while the FULL MOON rises, bathing everything in a silver phosphorescence.

                    RACHEL (V.O)
          - over a million pounds a year of DDT
          applied on citrus fields in California
          alone, enough to provide a lethal dose
          for five times the world's population.

Rachel stops reading. She notices a FIREFLY.

She goes OUTSIDE:

A FIREFLY circles her, then another. Louise's CAR approaches.
Rachel doesn't notice; she follows the fireflies to the
ocean. THUNDER AND LIGHTING. Scores of fireflies circle
over the reflection of the moon on the water, then around
Rachel as she wades in. She is ecstatic! Louise, in the
b.g., is mesmerized by Rachel's mysticism.

INT. DOCTOR'S OFFICE - BAR HARBOR - DAY

Rachel dresses. DOCTOR SAMUEL BRISKIN frowns as he looks at
her chest X-rays while he talks to a Colleague on the
telephone. Through the window, Rachel's POV: across the
street in a park, MARJORIE throws bread to the pigeons while
Rebecca happily runs after the pigeons, scattering them into
the air.

                    DR. BRISKIN
          Rachel. Well, I'm just a country doctor,
          and, well–

                    RACHEL
          – Rebecca is a beautiful girl.

                    DR. BRISKIN
          My dear Rachel, I don't know how to tell –

                    RACHEL
Samuel, you haven't read any new articles
on the effects of DDT on children –

                    DR. BRISKIN
– I'd feel a lot better if you saw Dr.
Caulk.

She ignores him, watching how happy Rebecca is.

                    DR. BRISKIN (cont'd)
Rachel.

                    RACHEL
Oh to be so young and free.

                    DR. BRISKIN
Promise me you'll see Dr. Caulk in
Washington.

INT. LOUISE AND SAM'S COTTAGE AT THE BIRD REFUGE – LATE AFTERNOON

The cottage: lots of books, cut flowers, Irish pine antiques, etc. Louise, Sam, and Maria play GIN RUMMY. Rachel serves hors d'oeuvres. Maria takes a swig of Sam's beer.

                    SAM
              (referring to Maria swigging
               his beer)
How do I know you ain't contaminated!

                    MARIA
You don't.

LOUISE
I've got news.

Rachel's POV: three Biplanes fly in formation over the nearby forest, release clouds of DDT.

MARIA
Good or bad?

LOUISE
Sam and I hired a lawyer. We don't care what anyone says, we're going to stop this awful DDT spraying.

MARIA
You don't have a chance in hell.

SAM
Wait and see, oh doubting one.

LOUISE
(interrupting Rachel's POV of the biplanes)
Rachel, come join our team.

RACHEL
Maybe I–

MARIA
– Not a chance in hell. She's got to take care of her old mama. Gin.

SAM
You're cheating again. Then we'll go after the bastards without you.

LOUISE
I know you're busy, but we need help, you're a scientist.

RACHEL
A B.A. in English, and an M.S. in biology, hardly an expert witness on chemical toxicity.

SAM
Say, what about getting your friend in the Ag. Department, what's his name – Eliot.

MARIA
It's bad enough that wild man is hounding her to write a damn book – imagine anyone interested in reading about PCT –

RACHEL
– DDT–

MARIA
– Whatever, that's what we taxpayers pay Eliot to do.

Rachel starts coughing, goes into the kitchen; Louise follows her.

RACHEL
Nobody'll listen to him.

MARIA
And what makes you think they'd pay you a second's attention?

IN THE KITCHEN:

Rachel can't stop coughing.

          LOUISE
A book? Did you tell Bill?

          RACHEL
I haven't decided for sure. I dropped him a note to see what he thought about the idea.

          LOUISE
But what about us, the trial? We could work together, it'd be fun.

          RACHEL
What good would I be? I'm a writer, not –

She can't stop coughing.

          LOUISE
You okay?

          RACHEL
Yes, it'll pass.

INT./EXT. RACHEL'S COTTAGE – DAY

ON THE SCREEN PORCH:

The ringing telephone wakes Rachel who has dozed off at her desk. Her POV: outside, Marjorie, wrapped in blankets, knitting, Maria painting. Rebecca enters as she records her dream in her journal.

RACHEL
(writing, looking overly
concerned)
...until a rain...a rain of death came...and the voices of spring were silent.

REBECCA
Telephone - what's wrong?

RACHEL
Nothing. Thank you Rebecca.

She answers the phone. While she talks, Rebecca climbs up in her lap, holds her.

BILL (ON PHONE)
What do you know about DDT or -

RACHEL
- Any of the other thousands of new chemicals they pour each year into the air, the water, the earth? Hello Bill, and how are you? -

BILL (ON PHONE)
- You've sold millions of books about the beauty of nature-

RACHEL
Now may hardly be the time for a carefree love of the planet.

MARIA
Rachel, come look.

REBECCA
Let me see, let me see.

Rebecca exits.

BILL (ON PHONE)
Promise me you'll give up this notion of American chemical companies poisoning–

RACHEL
– If I don't write about what's happening, who will?

BILL (ON PHONE.)
Okay, so you'll write a little something, what good–

RACHEL
– Listen, Bill, we've worked together for a number of years, but if I have to go to another publisher with this–

BILL (ON PHONE)
– Okay, all right, if you promise not to sound so preachy, for God's sake.
I'll contact some of the magazines that are always shouting anything from Miss Carson's desk, Reader's Digest, National Geo.

RACHEL
I may have to do a lot of work–

> BILL (ON PHONE)
> – But only an article; then back to your books. Let the Feds do their own housecleaning. Agreed?

> RACHEL
> My love to Ellen, and– Bill– thank you.

Rachel goes OUTSIDE:

Maria takes the binoculars away from Rebecca, hands them to Rachel.

> MARJORIE
> Due east, near the horizon.

Rachel's POV through the binoculars: a school of WHALES.

> MARIA
> You can't take on another project, you hear me!

> RACHEL
> They are beautiful, mamma.

INT. RACHEL'S COTTAGE - NIGHT

Everyone around the table on the porch, enjoying after dinner coffee, looking at Sam's PHOTOGRAPHS OF CHILDREN.

> RACHEL
> My children's book will be twice as wonderful with your photographs, Sam.

Sam hands Rachel a photo of Rebecca CHASING PUFFBALLS in a meadow.

SAM
This one of Rebecca is my favorite.

REBECCA
Let me see.

She grabs it out of his hand, tearing it.

RACHEL
Rebecca!

MARJORIE
Go to your room, right this minute.

REBECCA
It was an accident.

MARJORIE
Go!

REBECCA
I hate you. I'm glad you're going to die.

Rachel grabs Rebecca.

RACHEL
Rebecca, tell your mommy you don't mean–

Rebecca breaks away and exits, crying.

MARIA
That girl, what could be–

MARJORIE
It could be her father left us, it could be she's right, about me... "leaving"

No one knows quite what to say.

Sam hands Rachel a photo: CHILDREN climbing a BANYAN tree.

> SAM
> If Bill doesn't use this one, change publishers.

Rebecca falls in the hallway, whines.

> MARIA
> (referring to Rebecca)
> Rachel.

Rachel reluctantly goes to help Rebecca.

> LOUISE
> (referring to Sam's photo)
> At least you're good at something, Sam.

> MARIA
> Uh oh, now you two don't –

> MARJORIE
> (grabbing Rachel's hand)
> – No. I'll go. I'm tired anyway.

Marjorie exits after Rebecca.

> MARJORIE (cont'd)
> (to Rebecca)
> Don't cry Rebecca, don't cry, baby. Mama's sorry.

Rachel sees a car park in front, goes out to see.

MARIA
Now who could that be?

RACHEL
Eliot.

MARIA
What in the "h" does he want?

ELIOT
Careful Mrs. Carson, I heard that.

MARIA
Good.

Eliot takes a projector out of his truck.

RACHEL
You're just in time for a cup of Guatemalan coffee.

ELIOT
Sprayed with DDT – no thanks. I thought you all might enjoy a little government movie viewing to while away the night.

INT. RACHEL'S COTTAGE – LIVING ROOM – LATER

Horrified, they all watch a BLACK AND WHITE GOVERNMENT PROPAGANDA FILM about DDT and pesticides, etc. narrated by STEPHEN BLACK-ROBERTS, 47 – Director of Research, American Cyanamid Company, horn-rimmed glasses, scientist's white lab jacket, slight Harvard accent, condescending, pedantic.

While Black-Roberts, in a laboratory setting, speaks, the film is interspersed with the following scenes:

1. Ugly pictures, frightening ones, of various destructive insects:

>BLACK-ROBERTS (V.O.)
>For centuries, human beings have been forced to tolerate the destructive onslaught of various disease-carrying insects, like the mosquito which causes malaria, and sleeping sickness. Now–

2. Supertitle: "MIAMI: FIGHTING POLIO OUTBREAK", shots of OLD PEOPLE AND CHILDREN in IRON LUNGS, etc. in a hospital POLIO WARD, then CHILDREN at a school eating lunch as they happily get sprayed by clouds of DDT.

>MARIA
>You're wasting your precious time and God given talent if you think you can stop these people. Goodnight one and all.

>BLACK-ROBERTS
>...the war is on to conquer destructive and life threatening pests, including the dreaded plagues that have destroyed...

Rachel offers to wheel her, but she rebuffs her and exits.

>EVERYONE
>Night Maria.

>ELIOT
>You'll miss the best part.

3. Plague of grasshoppers in Kansas, a FARMER walking through his devastated CORNFIELD, millions of GRASSHOPPERS jumping all about. Segue into another CORNFIELD, green, thriving.

>   LOUISE
> This means you're definitely going to write the book.

>   BLACK-ROBERTS
> ...millions of acres of America's cropland.

Rachel nods "yes."

4. BLACK-ROBERTS lecturing to Secretary of Agriculture ORVILLE FREEMAN and GOVERNMENT OFFICIALS. He points to maps of the FIRE ANT "invasion" which turns into a cartoon Communist red ant invading America. Close up shots of real FIRE ANT MOUNDS, fire ants attacking a dead cow, fire ants swarming over a granary:

>   LOUISE
> Will you also have time to help Sam and I with the trial?

>   BLACK-ROBERTS (V.O.)
> ...Recently we've been invaded from countries South of the border by the dreaded red ant, which alone is a serious menace to America...

>   RACHEL
> I'll do my best.

Rachel holds her hand, but Louise pulls away.

>   ELIOT
> Our illustrious Secretary of Agriculture, Orville Freeman.

> LOUISE
> He's not bad looking.

> RACHEL
> For a Republican.

5. Dept. of Agriculture TRUCKS spray a herd of DAIRY COWS.

> SAM
> From now on, skip the milk in my coffee.

> ELIOT
> It's the American way, stop them before
> they stop you.

6. Army personnel and WW2 refugees sprayed with DDT from head to foot.

> RACHEL
> Did they stop the typhus outbreak?

> ELIOT
> Yeah, and thousands of G.I.'s have
> developed rare cancers and other
> mysterious ailments.

> LOUISE
> All we have to do is show this film to
> the jury, and we've won our case.

> RACHEL
> Something tells me it won't be so easy,
> darling.

ELIOT
(handing Rachel a Dept. of Ag.
document)
Here's your all-American "Proof" that the
fire ant, the mosquito, and the gypsy
moth were introduced in the
U.S. as part of a Communist conspiracy to
undermine the American food supply!

SAM
The Russians are coming, the big, bad
Russians!

The projector misfeeds, burns the film. Eliot tries to fix it, but the film starts burning on Black-Roberts' image:

RACHEL
Sabotage, no doubt.

ELIOT
You want to meet him?

LOUISE
Black-Roberts?

RACHEL
You're not serious?

EXT. CYANAMID CHEMICAL COMPANY - DAY

Eliot keeps switching the RADIO to get election results: (Kennedy may be losing, Nixon winning?, too close to call.)

ELIOT
If tricky Dicky Nixon wins, the chemical
companies get a blank check.

> RACHEL
> (referring to the trees along the road)
> So beautiful.

> ELIOT
> Until you turn the corner.

He turns off into the driveway to Cyanamid Chemical Co.: security guard entrance, chemical storage tanks dotting the riverside, white smoke belching into the air, etc.

> ELIOT (cont'd)
> Hold your breath.

> RACHEL
> How long?

EXT. CYANAMID CHEMICAL - DAY

FOYER: Through the picture window, Rachel watches WORKMEN (without protective gear) in the nearby fields spray toxic chemicals on test rows of crops. Eliot takes notes.

> BLACK-ROBERTS
> Eliot, what a surprise.

> ELIOT
> An unpleasant one, I hope.

> BLACK-ROBERTS
> Still sore about my making you look the fool in front of the Senate Ag Sub Committee?

> ELIOT
> Round one. Wait 'til I get you before the full committee.

                    BLACK-ROBERTS
          If, my dear Eliot, if. Shall we go in to
          my office?

They walk down the HALLWAY:

                    ELIOT
          I'd like you to meet my assistant, Rachel
          Carson: Robert Black-Roberts.

                    RACHEL
          Mr. Black –

                    BLACK-ROBERTS
          – Dr. Black-Roberts. My mother was an
          ardent suffragette; therefore Black,
          hyphen, Roberts. Assistant?

                    RACHEL
          Eliot's helping me with some research.
          Actually, I used to be his supervisor at
          the Department of Fish and Wildlife.

                    BLACK-ROBERTS
          Used to be. I see. Forgive me, but
          you're not *the* Rachel Carson?

They enter his OFFICE:

The office overlooks experimental field crop plots from one window, chemical manufacturing from another.

                    ELIOT
          Splendid view.

BLACK-ROBERTS
It's such an honor to meet the Grand
Authoress of the sea, though I imagined
you differently.

RACHEL
Taller, and carrying a scepter
like a female Poseidon no doubt. Sorry
to disappoint you.

BLACK-ROBERTS
Not at all. Here are the reports, all up
to date and in order, Eliot.
   (to Rachel)
I've read all your books to my children,
*The Sea Around Us, At the Edge of the
Sea.* We look forward to your next work.
More on the deep blue?

ELIOT
Yeah, seas of toxic blue–

BLACK-ROBERTS
– Miss Carson, I hope you're not one of
Eliot's Neanderthal au naturales.

GLORIA, 25, Black-Roberts' lonely secretary enters.

RACHEL
I hope not.

GLORIA
I thought you'd want to know: Nixon
finally conceded– Kennedy's won.

BLACK-ROBERTS
Damn.

                    RACHEL
          Wonderful.

                    ELIOT
          Thank God! Guess we'll get that hearing
          before the senate.

                    BLACK-ROBERTS (cont'd)
          How unfortunate. Well, what about a
          drink, to salute your new President and
          his rather handsome wife?

INT. BAR - ON A RIVER BANK - SUNSET

Rachel's POV: a COLLEGE ROWING TEAM races on the river past American Cyanamid Chemical smokestacks belching chemicals into the air. A JAZZ QUARTET plays in the b.g.

Gloria dances by herself. Eliot lusts after her, and vice versa.

                    BLACK-ROBERTS
          Maybe, perhaps, could be, doubtful, never
          happen! Miss Carson- are you familiar
          with Malthus' theory of population
          explosion -

                    ELIOT
          - Don't start.

                    RACHEL
          Yes, of course.

BLACK-ROBERTS
Sometime in the latter part of this century, there will be more than 250 million people in this grand country of ours. Gloria, come join us. You know Eliot.

RACHEL
How do you do, I'm Rachel Carson.

GLORIA
Charmed.

BLACK-ROBERTS
Two hundred and fifty million hungry red blooded Americans, Miss Carson – it is "Miss" I presume. Without pesticides and herbicides, forty percent of the population will have to go back to the farm so we can feed ourselves.

RACHEL
I remembering reading about farming experiments in France and Israel, where they've quadrupled food production, without chemical –

BLACK-ROBERTS
– Mere garden plots. You can't feed a nation on that.

GLORIA
I have my very own flower garden.
　(to Eliot)
Dance?

                    ELIOT
          Don't mind if I do.

They dance.

                    RACHEL
          People have managed to farm for thousands
          of years without pesticides.

                    BLACK-ROBERTS
          You'd have a hard time convincing our
          tomato farmers of that during the forties.

                    ELIOT
          The tomato blight was an anomaly. Tell
          Rachel about your own studies suggesting
          pesticides are cumulatively stored in the
          body's fatty tissue like –

                    BLACK-ROBERTS
          – the breast? But that was exposures
          hundreds of times –

                    FRANK THE BARTENDER
          – Dr. Black-Roberts, telephone.

                    BLACK-ROBERTS
          Excuse me. Frank, another round for Miss
          Carson, if you please.

He answers the phone at the bar. The Waiter gives Rachel her drink.

                    RACHEL
                (to the waiter)
          Thank you.

> BLACK-ROBERTS
> Actually, it's for you.

Rachel goes to answer the phone.

> BLACK-ROBERTS (cont'd)
> (toasting)
> Here's to progress and the American way.

Rachel, listening on the phone, FAINTS in SLOW-MOTION. NO SOUND. Her POV as she falls: a flock of WHITE BIRDS fly past the setting SUN through the smoke of the chemical factory.

EXT. PENNSYLVANIA COUNTRYSIDE - CARSON FARM - SUNSET

SLOW-MOTION: the Sun sets through LARGE RAIN DROPS that fall on MARJORIE'S CASKET as she is lowered into the ground.

Slowly, normal SOUND, end SLOW MOTION, as Maria takes Rebecca's hand. Louise comforts Rachel. Rebecca tosses dirt on the casket, then so do Maria, Sam, Louise, and Rachel.

EXT./INT. LIMOUSINE - TWILIGHT

Louise hugs Rachel. Maria and Rebecca wait in the limo.

> LOUISE
> I'll call when we get back to Boston.

Realizing Rebecca is next to Maria, Rachel gets in front.

> MARIA
> Come, sit with us. We're family now.

Rachel hesitates, then gets in back with them. Rebecca jumps into Rachel's arms, grabs her tight. Reluctantly, Rachel comforts her.

EXT. CLEAR LAKE, CALIF. - DAY

> RACHEL (V.O. WHILE TYPING)
> (reading aloud while typing)
> 1954. Clear Lake, California.

A lifeless lake, CHILDREN stare at bird carcasses:

> RACHEL (V.O. WHILE TYPING) (cont'd)
> In order to control the gnat population, the U.S. government applied DDT on Clear Lake's surface. Thousands of birds died.

INT. RACHEL CARSON'S HOUSE - NIGHT

She stops typing. She's tired. Her POV as she walks to her bedroom: candles in front of her Father's picture.

In her BEDROOM:

She gets in bed, turns off the light. Rebecca, half asleep, comes in, gets in bed, cuddles next to her. She doesn't quite know what to do.

INT./EXT. CAR - DAY

Pensive, Rachel drives along a tree-lined two lane blacktop, Rebecca is in back peering through binoculars. Periodically, Rachel rubs her sore neck.

> MARIA
> The elms are lovely.

Yellow throats fly by.

MARIA
Look at the pretty birds, Rebecca.

RACHEL
Yellow throats.

Rachel pulls over at gas station, next to a telephone booth.

RACHEL
I'm calling the college and telling them
I can't do it.

She gets out of the car, rubs her neck.

MARIA
Of course you can. Something wrong with
your neck?

She pulls out a fistful of nickels, dials.

RACHEL
I have more important work to do than
accept awards.

MARIA
Don't be ridiculous. Get in the car.

RACHEL
Thank you operator.

She puts in several nickels.

MARIA
Rachel, please. You always get a little
nervous before these kind of things.

RACHEL
I just don't feel right with all those literary lions.

MARIA
You've sold a hundred times more books than any of them! Stop acting like a child and get in.

REBECCA
A robin?

RACHEL
No, hermit thrush.

Rachel hangs up, gets into the car, drives off:

MARIA
The most beautiful of voices.

RACHEL
(to Rebecca)
There's a cardinal.
(to Maria)
It's their questions about transubstantiation, or how they really want to know my opinion about the social consequences of desegregation. I simply dissolve.

MARIA
If you can't tolerate people who admire you, how do you think you'll do against a government prosecutor if you testify for Sam and Louise.

                    RACHEL
          Hand me an aspirin please.

INT. RECEPTION ROOM – BOSTON COLLEGE – DAY

Too many people smoking, drinking, talking. Maria, next to a PORTRAIT of RACHEL as a female Poseidon, enjoys the limelight. Rachel, obviously not in her element, signs a copy of *The Sea Around Us* for a portly PROFESSOR.

                    PROFESSOR
          But don't you think the Negro situation
          demands at least as much attention as
          your love of nature?

                    RACHEL
          Yes, of course.

An Indian WRITER in a Nehru jacket:

                    WRITER
          Take care of one's self, and perhaps in
          the next life, one will have risen to the
          heights of taking care of others.

Bill Lakes rescues her.

                    BILL
          Excuse us, but if I don't twist Rachel's
          arm, I will never get the chapter she
          promised me, lo these many weeks ago.

                    WRITER
          God watch over you dear lady.

They walk outside into the rose garden courtyard.

EXT. ROSE GARDEN COURTYARD - SAME

Rebecca watches them through the window as they stroll.

> RACHEL
> Mother is enjoying herself.

> BILL
> This DDT thing, it could destroy your
> career. What makes you think Houghton -
> Mifflin will publish it?

> RACHEL
> You.

She sees Rebecca staring at her, her nose pressed against the window. ELLEN LAKES, 40, Bill's wife, athletic, confident, coaxes Rebecca away from the window.

> BILL
> You couldn't just let the chemists
> wrestle with this one?

She smiles at his suggestion. They go back inside -

INT. RECEPTION ROOM - SAME

- and join Ellen and Rebecca AT A BUTTERFLY COLLECTION, thousands of butterflies on pins. Rebecca CLINGS to Rachel.

> RACHEL
> I love the monarchs.

> ELLEN
> There must be thousands up near your
> place this time of year.

REBECCA
I ain't seen any.

RACHEL
Haven't. They've been spraying –

Louise and Sam enter.

BILL
– Louise, I was just thinking about you.

LOUISE
The final draft of my "Flowers and Friends" will be on your desk by yesterday.

BILL
Wasn't it Turgenev who said, "Writers write."

RACHEL
You remember Ellen, Bill's wife.

SAM
Best blueberry pie I've ever eaten.

LOUISE
Thanks a lot!

ELLEN
I'll have to make another next time we visit.

REBECCA
I know where blueberries grow.

ELLEN
Will you show me some time?

                    BILL
I was telling Rachel she'd better borrow
an armadillo skin if she takes on the
chemical companies, not to mention the
Feds.

                    SAM
Why Rachel, you're not a communist, are
you?

                    RACHEL
     (joking)
I turned in my card long ago.

                    LOUISE
"Rachel's like the mid-day sun
 Always very bright;
 Never stops her studying
 'Til she gets it right." Hamilton High
Yearbook
     (intentionally slurs the date)
19...

Rachel's embarrassed.

INT. RACHEL'S COTTAGE – NIGHT

BEDROOM:

Rachel packs. On t.v. in the front room, PRESIDENT KENNEDY, at a news conference, introduces TAFT BENSON, his new Secretary of Agriculture. She goes into the front room to turn it off. Maria is asleep in her wheelchair. Rachel covers her with a shawl.

                    MARIA
I was only dozing. Leave it on.

                    RACHEL
Kennedy appointed Taft Benson as the new
Secretary of Agriculture.

                    MARIA
That good?

                    RACHEL
I hope so.

                    MARIA
You really have to go tomorrow? Let
someone else save the world.

Rachel tries to kiss her, but Maria, angry, won't allow it.
Rachel exits. She goes into

Rebecca's ROOM:

She's kneeling at the side of her bed, talking to her Mother's
PICTURE in a 9X12 gold frame.

                    REBECCA
Yes, Auntie Maria is very nice to
me...Huh? Auntie Rachel?...I guess.

                    RACHEL
Rebecca, who are you talking to?

                    REBECCA
My Mamma.

EXT. TRAIN STATION – DAY

Louise and Sam get on the train. Rachel kisses Maria.

> MARIA
> I hope you know what you're doing.

> CONDUCTOR
> All aboard!

The train starts. Guilty, Rachel tries to kiss Rebecca, but she backs away.

> LOUISE
> Hurry Rachel!

> MARIA
> We'll be okay. Go.

Rachel catches up to the train. Sam holds out his hand for her. She hops on board, looks back at Maria trying to get Rebecca to wave to Rachel.

INT. MOVING TRAIN - EVENING

Sam, Louise, and Rachel dine as the sun sets.

> SAM
> It's crucial we get Eliot to testify.

> LOUISE
> So far we have several expert witnesses, an organic farmer who lost his entire strawberry crop-

> SAM
> - a dairy farmer-

> LOUISE
> - he had to slaughter his contaminated cows-

                    RACHEL
            – Look.

She motions to the sunset. They pause to watch. Sam points to BLOOD coming from Rachel's nose.

                    SAM
            Rachel.

                    RACHEL
            Excuse me.

She exits.

INT. TRAIN BATHROOM – EVENING

Louise enters, Rachel leans her head back to stop the bleeding. Louise helps her with the handkerchief.

                    LOUISE
            Maybe all this is a bit much.

                    RACHEL
            I'm more than a nanny and nurse. There's
            not enough–

                    LOUISE
            – Time?

EXT. HOUGHTON-MIFFLIN – BOSTON – RAINY DAY

In the b.g. Sam stands next to a hot dog VENDOR, eating a hot dog. Louise kisses Rachel. Rachel enters a revolving door.

INT. HOUGHTON-MIFFLIN – OFFICE- DAY

Rachel and Bill walk through the office busy with EDITORS.

BILL
This snake oil expert we retain as
council here knows his stuff.

YOUNG EDITOR
Mr. Lakes, I've...

BILL
Later Elaine. Someone's snooping around,
asking questions about your work.

RACHEL
Really? Who?

INT. CONFERENCE ROOM - DAY

RAYMOND SADLER, 50, Harvard blue blood, with Rachel and Bill in a wood paneled, plush conference room:

RAYMOND
Reader's Digest and five other magazines
all said thanks, but no thanks. We can
assume that a lot of people in high
places are "anxious" about your work and
have applied pressure to these various
publishing corporations.

RACHEL
They can't stop me from telling the truth.

RAYMOND
That I wouldn't wager on.

INT. ELEVATOR - DAY

> BILL
> I'll be damned if we'll let these House Un-American types tell us what to do.

> RACHEL
> Then you'll get my book published?

> BILL
> Houghton-Mifflin owes me a few.

INT. CONGRESSIONAL HEARING ROOM - WASHINGTON D.C. - DAY

Reporters, T.V. Crews, a packed Audience, and several Congressmen listen to Robert Black-Roberts, with his charts, enlarged photos of world famine- starving children, emaciated women, etc.

Rachel takes notes. Sam talks to a CONGRESSMAN. Louise talks to MARJORIE SPOCK, portly, close cropped hair, and MISS POLLY, her petite companion- withdrawn, sporting a shadowy (hormonal) mustache. EZRA TAFT-BENSON, the new Secretary of Agriculture, enters. Rachel notices Taft-Benson exchange a knowing look with Black-Roberts.

> BLACK-ROBERTS
> Do we in fact wish to shut down the most successful agricultural production the world has ever known because a few alarmists are unnecessarily concerned about possible health dangers "umpteen" years in the future?

> CONGRESSMAN
> Of course not Dr., however testimony
> before this committee suggests that
> possible health hazards to agricultural
> workers –

Black-Roberts continues as Eliot leans down behind Rachel.

> ELIOT
> Pick your poison – the new Secretary of
> Agrilculture, Taft Benson, or our front
> man from chemical hell.

> BLACK-ROBERTS
> If you will look at our report, sir, on
> page 45. My company, American Cynamid,
> has carefully researched those so-called
> DDT exposures and without exception, the
> occurences in question resulted from
> human error.

> RACHEL
> My God, Eliot, it's much worse than I
> ever imagined.

> BLACK-ROBERTS
> Now I ask you, we don't shut down the
> steel industry, nor do we put a halt to
> the assembly lines in Detroit, every
> time a worker makes a mistake...

The SERGEANT-AT-ARMS scowls at Rachel and Eliot with a "be quiet" look. They make their way outside:

> ELIOT
> You're getting too thin.

> RACHEL
> (nodding to hefty Taft-Benson)
> But D.C.'s fatter than ever.

> ELIOT
> Our new Secretary of Agriculture? It's
> his patriotic duty to appreciate good
> food!

A WOMAN in the GALLERY points to Rachel, asks her FRIEND:

> WOMAN
> Isn't that Rachel Carson?

INT. CONGRESSIONAL HALLWAY - BLACK-ROBERTS - DAY

A CROWD, some carrying protest signs. Across the hall, a MOTHER holds her BABY while she leans against the door to another Hearing Room. RACHEL'S POV: inside the hearing room, a DEFENSE FILM on nuclear testing, a HYDROGEN BOMB CLOUD exploding.

> ELIOT
> I've spent the last week and a half
> testifying before this god-forsaken
> committee - documenting the poisoning of
> twenty-three various crops.

FRAN ROBERTSON, behind a widow's veil, shyly approaches.

> FRAN ROBERTSON
> I'm Fran Robertson. Could you help me?
> Since they sprayed our elm trees with
> DDT, I'm from Illinois, the birds, all
> the birds have –

MRS. WALLER, red cheeked, with a distinct New York accent.

> MRS. WALLER
> – What about our dairy farm, we can't sell our milk!

> ELIOT
> Did you report –

> MRS. WALLER
> – They shut us down. We begged them not to spray, showed them proof there weren't any gypsy moth near our area.

MR. PARKER, a wiry old man, with a broadbrimmed hat:

> MR. PARKER
> Name's Parker, from Norfolk, Connecticut. Same with my bees, killed dead after them damn DDT aeroplanes –

> RACHEL
> – Surely, Eliot, there's something –

> ELIOT
> Maybe your book; I've done my bit.

Louise enters with MRS. SPOCK and MISS POLLY.

> RACHEL
> Mr. Parker, will you write to me? And you too ma'am. Maybe–

LOUISE
– Rachel, I'd like you to meet Mrs. Spock, she's the brave soul suing the government to stop the spraying. We're partners.

MRS. SPOCK
Glad to have you on our side. This is Miss Polly.

Miss Polly manages a nod.

RACHEL
How do you do? Eliot–

ELIOT
You're the not-so-little lady ready to storm the castle of progress.

MRS. SPOCK
Bitter, but amusing. I like that. We hear you will testify at our trial.

ELIOT
Excuse us for a moment. Rachel.

People exit the hearing room as Eliot pulls Rachel aside.

MRS. SPOCK
Certainly, in fact Miss Polly and I have a train to catch. Good to meet you, one and all.

RACHEL
Likewise.

Louise escorts Mrs. Spock and Miss Polly out, miming to Rachel "see you later."

> ELIOT
> What's all this about my testifying!?

> RACHEL
> They asked me to ask you.

> ELIOT
> Okay you asked. The answer is no.

> RACHEL
> They need your help.

> ELIOT
> How's about a drink instead?

INT. MOVING CAR - COUNTRY HIGHWAY - NIGHT

> ELIOT
> At least you had the good sense to quit and write a few best-sellers.

> RACHEL
> To tell the truth, I miss working at Fish and Wildlife.

He stops the car.

> ELIOT
> This ought to give you a little inspiration.

EXT. PATUXENT CHEMICAL PITS - NIGHT

They get out of the car. The wind howls, then suddenly stops. It is absolutely quiet. A sign: "NO TRESPASSING. CHEMICAL CONTAMINATION." He turns the car lights on: the landscape looks like the surface of the moon.

> ELIOT
> Welcome to the future now, Patuxent, Maryland, a chemical wasteland. It was here that DDT got its "umpf", chlordane, its "zip", dieldrin, its "zap"- a virtual-

> RACHEL
> - rain of death.

> ELIOT
> You are the poet.

He leads her through a hole in the fence. They walk, stop, listen. It's dead quiet. Because of the stench, Eliot gives her a hanky to cover her nose.

> RACHEL
> Why the stench?

> ELIOT
> The smell of death-by-progress- get used to it. Let's get the hell out of here.

INT. PFAFF'S COFFEE HOUSE - NIGHT

Beatnik coffee house, serving beer & wine, jazz, and poetry. Rachel and Eliot, in a backroom looking out on the Beat scene, rifle through papers. Eliot dances with himself while they talk. In the b.g. two Beatnik poets read their poetry accompanied by a JAZZ QUARTET.

> RACHEL
> This is good, Eliot.

> ELIOT
> Yeah, after I submitted it, they sent me to Oregon for six months to count the salmon runs. One fishy, two fishy.

> RACHEL
> At least you got the Department of Agriculture to pay attention to its own toxicity studies.

> ELIOT
> You mean the heptachlor scare? Hell, when half the population of an area the size of Wisconsin gets the runs, even Big Brother takes notice. This report
>   (He hands her another folder)
> got me my all expenses paid sojourn to the Everglades, during mosquito season, to study the mating habits of alligators, or was it crocodiles?

They listen to the Poets:

> POET #1
> I saw my best friends taken by madness, impoverished, crazy –

> POET #2
> – beat poets starving for the celestial soul of solitude.

> RACHEL
>   (referring to the folder)
> It gets worse?

ELIOT
"Perverse worse." Every American mother tested, from Florida to Montana, shows breast tissue and breast milk contamination.

RACHEL
My God Eliot.

POET #1
– Who were driven from the universities for crazy and writing obscene ditties on the windows of the skull, oh Allah, Allah!

POET #2
Oh Angel of Darkness! Oh Ticky-tacky apartments! Spectre of suburbs! Atomic industries!

AUDIENCE
Go, man, go!

POET #1 AND POET #2
Who sang out of their darkness in despair, buried alive in their innocent flannel suits on Madison Avenue amid blasts of nitroglycerine and mustard gas of sinister editors run down by the drunken nowhere of day to day.

The coffee house CROWD claps. The JAZZ QUARTET plays a slow number.

RACHEL
Why is the government –

ELIOT
Where there's money... Come on, let's dance.

RACHEL
I'm afraid my dancing days are over.

ELIOT
Nobody says no to Glen Miller!

They dance, laughing, but she easily tires and sits down; Eliot keeps on dancing.

INT. SCIENTIST'S OFFICE - DAY

Eliot answers the phone while the Secretary, in the outer office, straightens her nylons (for his benefit).

RACHEL (V.O. ON PHONE)
Can you get me names of the scientists currently experimenting with DDT, chlordane, and lindane?

ELIOT (cont'd)
Don't forget benzene, adenosine, and triphosphate.
    (He closes the door so the
    Secretary can't hear.)
And no, I won't give you names.

RACHEL (V.O. ON PHONE)
Why not?

ELIOT
Because I haven't sprayed the phone for bugs yet!

He hangs up.

INT. RACHEL'S SILVER SPRINGS, MARYLAND HOME – NIGHT

Miles Davis on the phonograph: Eliot sketches a picture of Rachel HOLDING UP THE WORLD. Sam and Louise and Rachel go over notes, share a drink. Eliot gives Rachel the drawing.

>   RACHEL
> You should have been an artist.
>
>   ELIOT
>   (be-boping to Miles Davis)
> Should of, could of been a writer. Should a, could-a.

He tries to get Rachel to dance, but she begs off.

>   ELIOT (cont'd)
> Louise?

He doesn't let Louise say no. They dance.

>   LOUISE
> I guess I don't mind if I do.
>
>   RACHEL
> Remember, she's a married woman.
>
>   SAM
> That's what I'm always telling her.
>
>   RACHEL
> What about toxicity tests on DDT?
>
>   ELIOT
> Classified. Commies and all that.

SAM
Can we get copies of these for evidence?

LOUISE
(referring to Eliot's dancing)
And I here I always thought chemistry was boring.

ELIOT
The really nasty stuff is kept under lock and key. Some at Fish and Wildlife, most at Patuxent. Want to see it?

Rachel grabs Eliot's hat, her sweater, and escorts him out.

RACHEL
Excuse us.

ELIOT
We going somewhere?

RACHEL
Fish and Wildlife.

LOUISE
Should we wait up?

INT. FISH AND WILDLIFE - NIGHT

Flashlight in hand, Eliot and Rachel exit his office, walk down the hallway. We see PICTURES on the wall of Rachel and Eliot, much younger, working in a farm field, Rachel receiving an award, etc. Eliot opens a door into a dark hallway. They walk down the hallway. He shines his light on a door marked "Restricted Entry." They enter.

INT. WAREHOUSE – NIGHT

Rachel turns on the light. Before her is a KAFKAESQUE FOOTBALL FIELD size warehouse with endless stacks of paper, file cabinets, books, etc.

          ELIOT
    Somewhere in our little menagerie are a
    few thousand reports that might, just
    might mind you, help you bring the
    chemical boys back to reality.

Above each section are various signs: "Nazi Gas Experiments, World War 1, toxicity" etc.

          RACHEL
    World War 2, Germany, what's this?

          ELIOT
    A lot of these pesticides started out as
    one or another chemical warfare
    experiment. When the war ended, I guess
    they thought it was a shame to let all
    that good poison go to waste.

He opens the file cabinet. She looks through the files while he opens another file drawer.

          ELIOT (cont'd)
    Here it is. You remember Jake Rotham?

          RACHEL
    Handsome Jake, Fish and Wildlife's most
    brilliant scientist, present company
    excepted.

                    ELIOT
            Was. He blew the whistle. He's managing a
            wildlife park now, somewhere in nowhere
            West Texas.

A NOISE from the other side of the room. They freeze, then Rachel sees a cat.

                    RACHEL
            The culprit.

She picks up the cat. Eliot unlocks a caged area marked "Classified." He opens a cabinet, hands Rachel a file.

                    ELIOT
            You wanted names.

She copies names while Eliot thumbs through files.

                    ELIOT (cont'd)
            Here's something from your neck of the
            woods: Maine gypsy moth.

She takes the file. They freeze when they hear a DOOR close, see a FLASHLIGHT moving past the windows outside. The door opens: it's TOM, the nightguard.

                    TOM
            Sweetpea, where are you girl?

                    ELIOT
            Evening Tom.

TOM
Oh it's you Doc. I saw the light,
thought maybe Sweetpea here was up to no
good.
   (to Rachel)
Evening.

ELIOT
Rachel, meet Tom Johnson, guardian of all
that meets the eye.

TOM
Yeah, guardian of dust.

RACHEL
Good to meet you Tom. Who's Sweetpea?

He writes down Rachel's name.

TOM
My cat. Miss Carson, huh. Well, don't
let me interrupt you all's work.
   (to Sweetpea)
Come on precious, chow time. God knows
why you two are interested in this stuff;
they've been shredding it lately like
there's no tomorrow.

ELIOT
Night Tom.

TOM
You folks might see a little easier if
you turned on the lights.

ELIOT
Trying to save the taxpayers a few bucks,
Tom.

>   TOM
>   That'll be the day.

Tom exits with the cat.

EXT. RACHEL CARSON'S SILVER SPRINGS HOME – NIGHT

POV of a STRANGER, behind a tree, taking PHOTOGRAPHS through the window of: Eliot is standing on his head in a Yoga position; Rachel types. IDA, 50, diminutive, Rachel's housekeeper enters with tea.

INT. RACHEL CARSON'S SILVER SPRINGS HOME – SAME

>   RACHEL
>   Thank you Ida.
>
>   IDA
>   Honey? Lemon?

Rachel nods yes.

>   RACHEL
>   (reading from her manuscript)
>   The "control of nature" is a phrase
>   conceived in arrogance born in a
>   Neanderthal Age of philosophy when it was
>   supposed that Nature exists for the
>   convenience of men and women.

She looks at Ida for approval, but Ida frowns. Rachel strikes out the last two words ("and women").

>   RACHEL (cont'd)
>   "for the convenience of men"– period.

Ida nods agreement, exits. Rachel types, stops– something outside catches her attention. She walks to the window. Eliot stops his Yoga, pours himself a drink, drinks it and gets into another Yoga position.

          RACHEL (cont'd)
Eliot.

          ELIOT
Not now Rachel, I'm communicating with your God.

PHONE RINGS. Rachel doesn't see anything outside. She answers the phone.

          RACHEL
Hello?
  (Pause)
Hello?

          MARIA (ON PHONE)
Say hello.

          RACHEL
Rebecca? You okay?

          REBECCA (ON PHONE)
When are you coming home?

          RACHEL
Soon.

          MARIA (ON PHONE)
Hello Rachel. How's the house?

RACHEL
The stains in the rug are gone, the
drapes are immaculate, Ida's a leprechaun
from Heaven. Is everything all right,
Mamma?

MARIA (ON PHONE)
Rebecca wanted to say good night, that's
all. She's got the sniffles, nothing to
worry about.

RACHEL
You sure?

MARIA (ON PHONE)
I better get her back to bed. Say good
night Rebecca.

Sam and Louise enter. They see Eliot in a contorted Yoga position: Sam raises his eyebrows and heads for the bar.

SAM
What did you do to the poor fellow?

REBECCA (ON PHONE)
No.

RACHEL
Rebecca—

MARIA (ON PHONE)
— Good night Rachel.

Upset, she hangs up.

LOUISE
Anything wrong?

EXT. RACHEL'S SILVER SPRINGS HOME – LATER

The Stranger takes more photographs: Rachel photographs secret photographs. Sam rifles through several files, hands one to Louise, another to Rachel. Eliot pours himself a drink.

INT. RACHEL'S SILVER SPRINGS HOME – SAME

          ELIOT
      (drunk)
Anyone want a drink?
      (no one answers)
Don't mind if I do.

          SAM
      (referring to files in Eliot's
      open briefcase)
What have we here?

          ELIOT
Sorry pal, top secret.

Eliot tries to grab the file, but Sam tosses it to Louise.

          SAM
What if I subpoenaed them?

          LOUISE
Or they just disappeared?

          ELIOT
Who do you want to see in prison, them or you?

Louise stuffs the file in her suit jacket, but Eliot wrestles it away from her. DOOR BELL RINGS. Everyone quickly starts putting the folders away.

          RACHEL
Ida, will you answer that dear?

          ELIOT
You know damn well if I testify for you, I'll get fired.

          LOUISE
We've got a son of a bitch for a lawyer – Susan Hinds.

Ida goes to answer the door.

          ELIOT
Never heard of her. And you'll wish you never had.

          SAM
What do you mean?

          ELIOT
You think our government, God bless their self-righteous soul, is going to let you convict them of poisoning every man, woman, and child, not to mention the precious little birdies?

          SAM
Then we'll go after the chemical companies.

          ELIOT
It's the government who greases the chemical companies' wheels, stupid.

CHERYL STANFORD, Eliot's gracious wife, enters.

>RACHEL
>How good to see you Cheryl!

>CHERYL
>The years, my God.

>RACHEL
>They've been kind to you.

>ELIOT
>Come on in and join the party. Look at these puffed up folks. Wait until the F.B.I. gets through with them, or maybe the I.R.S., huh Sam? Got any money under your mattress?

>CHERYL
>The boys are asleep in the car.

>SAM
>Look Eliot, we know it's an uphill battle.

>ELIOT
>Uphill, down hill, straight to hell.

>RACHEL
>Really Eliot.

>CHERYL
>We shouldn't leave the boys alone. Say good night.

                    ELIOT
    Really Rachel. They're going to crush us
    like a bug. Goodnight.

He and Cheryl exit.

                    LOUISE
    Well, at least he can dance.

INT. DR. GEORGE CAULK'S OFFICE - DAY

DR. GEORGE CAULK- elderly, Albert Einstein hair- enters his office. Rachel finishes dressing while looking at his medical library.
                    RACHEL
    Ever come across studies on chemical
    toxicity and cancer?

                    DR. CAULK
    Yes, there's some work on that at Harvard
    and at Berkeley, if memory serves me.

                    RACHEL
    I've recently come to terms with an
    idea that I'm now convinced will be an
    important book.

                    DR. CAULK
    I look forward to it.
        (Pause)
    There are two tumors, Rachel, one is benign.

                    RACHEL
    And the other?

                    DR. CAULK
          I recommend surgery. You'll have to move
          back to D.C. for a while.

                    RACHEL
          But Mamma is so comfortable in Maine.

                    DR. CAULK
          The sooner the better.

INT. DEPARTMENT STORE - DAY

Two BOYS play mock WAR as Rachel looks at toys: guns, tanks, planes, toy soldiers. She's disappointed. Finally, she sees paints and an easel.

INT./EXT. RACHEL'S SILVER SPRINGS HOME - DAY

Rachel enters with Rebecca's easel. On the record player: Mario Lanza singing Italian love songs.

                    RACHEL
          Louise? Sam?

No answer. She sees a letter from Rebecca and opens it. It is her drawing of a sea anemone. She is touched. She goes to her

BEDROOM:

Louise and Sam are asleep, naked, on the floor. It's obvious they have been lovemaking. Louise wakes, gives Rachel a coy smile, then closes the door. Rachel goes into the

FRONT ROOM:

and, angrily, starts typing.

>   RACHEL (V.O.) (cont'd)
>   Dear Professor Riley: I am writing a
>   book about environmental contamination.

Rachel stops typing. She goes outside into the

BACKYARD:

She enters the orchid greenhouse and starts filling orchid pots with soil. Louise calls to her from the porch:

>   LOUISE
>   Rachel? Rachel?

Rachel doesn't answer. She's trying to hold back her tears.

INT. TRAIN – DAY

In silence, Rachel and Sam make notes from their DDT folders. Louise enters with drinks. Through the train window: migrating geese in the distance.

>   LOUISE
>   Lucky devils.

>   SAM
>   What do you say we all follow them south
>   next year, after you've finished your
>   book?

Rachel starts crying.

>   LOUISE
>   Rachel?

>   RACHEL
> I have to have an operation.
>
>   LOUISE
> Cancer?

Rachel doesn't answer.

>   LOUISE (cont'd)
> No, no, please, no.

Rachel doesn't answer. Louise becomes hysterical.

>   LOUISE (cont'd)
> But the trial, and your book. Isn't there
> something-
>
>   RACHEL
> Excuse me.

Rachel exits.

>   SAM
> For Christ's sake Louise, what's wrong
> with you?

INT. RACHEL'S MAINE COTTAGE - NIGHT

Rachel puts down the easel she bought for Rebecca. She's asleep. Rachel looks at her, how beautiful she is. She starts to stroke Rebecca's hair, but decides not to.

>   MARIA (O.S.)
> Rachel?

She goes into Maria's room.

MARIA (cont'd)
I'm so glad you're home

They embrace. Rachel notices medicine.

RACHEL
You okay?

MARIA
A touch of flu.

Rachel knows she's lying.

EXT. SEASHORE NEAR RACHEL'S COTTAGE –DAY

Bill and Rachel walk along the shore. Rebecca is up ahead with Ellen, tossing a football.

RACHEL
The heart of the argument is in the long term exposure to people– and other living things.

BILL
Houghton-Mifflin is not delighted with my recommendation to go ahead with the book.

RACHEL
Will they publish it or not?

BILL
I've tried to convince them it will be a monumental achievement. Will it?

Rebecca runs after a blue heron, shouting to Ellen:

                    REBECCA
          Great blue heron!

She looks at Rachel for approval. Rachel nods yes.

                    RACHEL
          Ellen's so good with Rebecca.

                    BILL
          You really think you can write a book
          about pesticides someone will want to
          read?

                    RACHEL
          Children are more at risk than adults! If
          we continue to indiscriminately use these
          chemicals–

                    BILL
          – Okay, okay. If we're wrong about this,
          I can always go back to my great American
          novel.

They shake. Bill catches the football and joins Ellen and Rebecca. Rachel watches, in pain.

EXT. RACHEL'S COTTAGE – DAY

Rachel pours lemonade in glasses around the picnic table while Bill adds logs to the fire pit.

                    RACHEL
          There's something else.

                    BILL
          Don't tell me you're going to write a book
          on the evils of nuclear pollution!

>RACHEL
>It had crossed my mind. Promise me...if something should happen, you'll see to it that Mamma and Rebecca...

Everyone claps when Ellen enters with a hot blueberry pie, followed by Rebecca who's obviously been helping her bake.

>SAM
>The Queen of Blueberries.

>MARIA
>Come and get it. Chemical stew!

They all sit at the table.

>ELLEN
>Where's Louise?

>RACHEL
>She's a little under the weather.

>SAM
>Yeah, weak heart, no spine.

Ellen motions for everyone to wait.

>ELLEN
>Wait one second.
>   (to Rebecca)
>You ready?

Ellen mouths the words as Rebecca speaks, which pleases Rachel.

>   REBECCA
> We love our bread, we love our butter,
> but most of all we love each other.

INT. RACHEL'S HOUSE - NIGHT

Walking down the hall, Rachel sees Rebecca, in her pajamas, painting in her bedroom. She enters.

>   RACHEL
> Time for sleep.

She doesn't want Rachel to see her painting (of a hospital), but Rachel does before she turns off the light, and gets into bed. Rachel tucks her in, leans down to kiss her.

>   REBECCA
> You going away again?

>   RACHEL
> I may have to.

She turns over, mad. Rachel enters

MARIA'S BEDROOM.

Maria is reading Rachel's text.

>   MARIA
> Your book. It's too technical. Urethane
> Isoprophyl-N-Phenyl-Carbamate, the
> halogenated aliphatic olefinic- it reads
> like a god damn chemistry text.

                    RACHEL
          I'm going to bed.

She kisses Maria goodnight. Maria grabs Rachel's hand.

                    MARIA
          Your Dr. Caulk called. We're a fine pair,
          me in my wicker throne, you...

Maria and Rachel hold each other.

INT. HOSPITAL - OPERATING ROOM, WASHINGTON D.C.- DAY

Rachel's blurred POV: Dr. Caulk, surrounded by team of NURSES, DOCTORS, etc. Behind the glare of operating room flood lights, is the ghost of Rachel's FATHER. He motions for her to come with him. She closes her eyes.

BLACK SCREEN.

EXT. PENNSYLVANIA FARM COUNTRY - MOVING CAR - NIGHT

FADE IN:

Forty years earlier. RACHEL, 6, sits next to her Father who is driving. Maria, forty years younger, asleep as they drive down the dark country two lane blacktop. Rachel's father stops, gets out of the car.

                    RACHEL
          Papa?

>   RACHEL'S FATHER
> Come on Rachel, it's time you heard the
> heavenly music.

He holds out his hand for her. She hops out of the car. It is a WINDY, PARTLY-CLOUDY, COLD night. They walk.

>   RACHEL'S FATHER (cont'd)
> We have to say a little prayer.

They stop. When he looks at her, Rachel TRANSFORMS INTO Rebecca.

>   REBECCA
> Okay.

>   RACHEL'S FATHER
> Close your eyes.

Rebecca repeats phrase after phrase:

>   REBECCA AND RACHEL'S FATHER
> "Hands above your head, hands gently on
> top of your head, hands gently on your
> eyes, hands gently on your ears, hands
> gently on your mouth, give yourself a
> nice hug, a gentle pat, palms together,
> now it's time to say danke, and merci and
> domo arigato."

As they pray, the clouds clear. Rebecca opens her eyes:

A STARRY, STARRY NIGHT.

INT. DOCTOR'S HOSPITAL WASHINGTON D.C. - DAY

Waking from surgery, Rachel's BLURRED POV: Rebecca's face. She is in the corner of the room, sulking. Maria is talking, but Rachel can't make out what she is saying.

>   RACHEL
> Rebecca.

>   MARIA
> Rachel, you're all right now, the doctor said.

Rachel reaches for Rebecca's hand, but she won't take it. Louise, crying, puts a pot of HYACINTHS on the table. She can't stand seeing Rachel in pain. She exits.

>   SAM
> Louise! God damn it woman.

He goes after her. Behind them is the ghost of Rachel's father who smiles, then VANISHES. Rachel tries to talk.

>   RACHEL
> Life, Rebecca.

At the door:

>   LOUISE
>   (hysterical)
> We have to meet the lawyers. I told you, my mother suffered so, I'm sorry, it's better this way.

She runs out.

>   SAM
> I'm sorry Rachel.

                    MARIA
          Poets!

As he exits, he bumps into Eliot carrying several folders.

                    ELIOT
          Enough damaging material - names,
          experiments, dates, etc., etc. - to keep
          you busy for a while.

                    RACHEL
               (too weak to talk)
          Thank-

                    ELIOT
          - Thank me with a dance.

INT. RACHEL'S SILVER SPRING HOME - DAY
FRONT ROOM:

Ida helps Rebecca with her raincoat. Maria hands her her book satchel. The school bus honks O.S.

                    MARIA
          Mind the teacher, speak when spoken to,
          wash your hands after-

                    RACHEL (V.O.)
          Rebecca.

RACHEL'S BEDROOM:

Ida leads Rebecca to Rachel's door. Rachel is very weak.

>   IDA
> Give your auntie a kiss.

O.S. the school bus honks again. She runs away.

>   MARIA (V.O.)
> Rebecca!

INT. HOSPITAL - RADIATION ROOM - DAY

Radiation warning LIGHT blinks as Rachel watches the huge radiaton machine whirl surrealistically about her.

INT. RACHEL'S SILVER SPRINGS HOME - DAY

Maria reads Sam's letter to Rachel, in bed. Rachel's hair has thinned (from the radiation treatments). Maria picks hair off her pillow and discards it. Rachel's POV: through the bedroom window: Rebecca outside, forlorn, sitting under a tree.

>   MARIA
> Louise likes the lawyer, Susan Hinds,
> thinks she's doing just fine.
>   (reading the Louise's letter)
> "With all the information to digest,
> Hinds focused right in on the major
> issues- the right of the people to know
> if they are being poisoned, the right to
> stop the poisoning" etc. "Basically, if
> Eliot's testimony is as strong as we
> hope, we have a good shot at stopping
> them- " if she's such a good friend, why
> the hell isn't she here!

> RACHEL
> Her mother suffered so long, so much from
> her cancer. It hurts Louise to see me
> like this. Besides, she's doing the work
> I should.

Phone RINGS. Maria exits to answer it. Rachel puts on her glasses, tries to read the letter. Her eyes hurt, she rubs them, reads, closes her eyes, appears to doze off.

OUTSIDE: Rebecca seems alarmed when Rachel dozes off. She presses his face close to the window and taps. No response.

She runs INTO RACHEL'S ROOM from outside. She waits, cautiously, reaches out to touch her, to see if she is dead.

> RACHEL (cont'd)
> Hello.

She is startled. She starts to leave.

> RACHEL (cont'd)
> Before you go, do me a favor?

She stops, but doesn't answer.

> RACHEL (cont'd)
> Will you feed the birds for me?

> REBECCA
> I can't reach the bird house.

> RACHEL
> Come here.

She hesitates.

                    RACHEL (cont'd)
          Please.

She gives in. Rachel whispers in her ear.

INT. RACHEL'S SILVER SPRINGS HOME - DUSK

Birds singing outside so loud they wake Rachel. Rachel's POV: Rebecca outside standing like a statue, both her outstretched hands full of bird seed: scores of birds flock around her, one or two birds feed from her hands.

INT. HOSPITAL - DAY

Dr. Caulk examines Rachel as she lays on a table. He gives a reassuring smile, exits. Behind a window, a NURSE TECHNICIAN prepares the chemo drip. Dr. Caulk and the Nurse exit. Rachel watches the chemo drip, drip.

EXT./INT. RACHEL'S SILVER SPRINGs HOME - EVENING

Sam and Louise get out of their car, walk up to the house.

Louise's POV: Rachel in her bedroom, sitting in front of her mirror, combing a wig. Rachel is almost completely bald. Rachel tries to stand up, but can't. She reaches for her cane and struggles up. Exhausted, she sits back down. Louise, tears streaming down her face, stops Sam.

                    LOUISE
          I can't. Not yet.

She goes back to the car. Sam gives up in desperation.

INT. RACHEL'S SILVER SPRINGS HOME - LATER

Rebecca and Maria at THANKSGIVING table. Ida brings in the turkey. Jeffie, the cat, hops on the table.

                    MARIA
          Watch your manners, Jeffie.

Rachel, using a cane, enters. Rebecca gets up to help Rachel into her chair.

                    MARIA (cont'd)
          You sure you're-

                    RACHEL
          - Can't stay in bed forever.
                    (to Rebecca)
          Thank you darling.
                    (to Maria)
          I guess Sam and Louise couldn't make it after all.

                    MARIA
          I guess not. Rebecca, will you say grace?

Rebecca hesitates.

                    RACHEL
          Please.

                    REBECCA
          Hands above your head, hands gently on
          top of your head, hands gently on your
          eyes, hands gently on your ears, hands
          gently on your mouth, give yourself a
          nice hug, a gentle pat, palms together,
          now it's time to say danke, and merci and
          domo arigato.

> RACHEL
> Thank you.

INT. RACHEL'S BACK PORCH SILVER SPRINGS HOME - DAY

Rachel types, but her hands ache. Her POV: the gentle SNOW falling outside. Maria and Rebecca paint the snow covered backyard. Maria notices Rachel is having difficulty typing. Maria wheels over to Rachel, takes the typewriter from her.

> RACHEL
> But I have so much–

> MARIA
> – So dictate, I used to do sixty words a minute.

> RACHEL
> I thought you didn't approve.

> MARIA
> I don't.

Rachel dictates while Maria types:

> RACHEL
> One must ask the question: Are pesticides and herbicides responsible for environmental diseases? It has been proven that they foul the soil, the water...

> MARIA
> – contaminate soil...

                    RACHEL
          Contaminate the soil, water, and food,
          that they soon will make our rivers
          fishless, our forests and parks birdless.
          We must finally recognize that Man is
          part of nature, not Master over earth.
          We must stop pretending that we can avoid
          the poisons with which we have
          contaminated the earth
                (Maria smiles)
          ...and that threatens life itself...

INT. RACHEL'S SILVER SPRINGS HOME - NIGHT

Rachel enters Rebecca's bedroom, looks at her in bed, notices
a photo of herself in the corner of the gold frame with Rebecca's
Mother's picture.

                    REBECCA
          Promise you won't go away again?

                    RACHEL
          Promise.

She kisses her goodnight. She enters the FRONT ROOM and
dials the telephone.

                    RACHEL (cont'd)
          Louise?

                    LOUISE (ON PHONE)
          Rachel? You all right?

                    RACHEL
          I'm better, a little thinner.

                    LOUISE (ON PHONE)
          You are brave.

                    RACHEL
          Not really.

                    LOUISE (ON PHONE)
          It's just that my mother suffered...
          forgive me for not being with
          you.

                    RACHEL
          Come for Christmas. Please.

                    LOUISE (ON PHONE)
          We're so busy preparing for the trial.
          You understand.

                    RACHEL
          Yes, of course.

INT. HOSPITAL - DAY

Rachel undergoes more chemo treatment.

INT. SILVER SPRINGS HOME - DAY - CHRISTMAS EVE

Cheery Christmas mantle, bright Christmas tree. Rachel corrects her manuscript. She looks anxious, looking out the window for Louise and Sam to arrive. Rebecca plays with a Mr. Potato Head. Maria is typing.

                    MARIA
          Damn Louise. I wouldn't hold my breath if
          I were you.

                    RACHEL
          She'll come.

Ida enters with hot cider which she serves to Rebecca.

                    IDA
          Here you are Rebecca. Should we still
          wait?

                    MARIA
          Rachel?

                    RACHEL
          I guess not.

Doorbell rings.

EXT. RACHEL'S SILVER SPRINGS HOME - SAME

Louise is still in the car, Sam rings the doorbell.

                    SAM
          Louise!

                    LOUISE
          Please Sam.

                    SAM
          We're not leaving until-

Rachel opens the door.

                    RACHEL
          Sam.

Sam kisses Rachel. Rachel's POV: Louise, ashamed, in the car. Rachel walks, with her cane, toward Louise. It is very painful and difficult for Rachel. She pauses, Louise gets out of the car, walks toward Rachel. Rachel walks toward Louise, slips, Louise catches her. They hug, cry, kiss.

    SAM
Merry Christmas, one and all.

INT. RACHEL'S SILVER SPRINGS HOME - LATER

Ida enters, dressed as Santa Claus, carrying presents.

    IDA
Ho ho, Merry Christmas.

    LOUISE
Merry Christmas.

    REBECCA
Un't uh, not until tomorrow.

    SAM
I think it came a little early this year.

He hands Rebecca a big model airplane.

    RACHEL
What do you say?

    REBECCA
Thank you, can I open my other presents?

    RACHEL
Go ahead. The big one is from me.

She enthusiastically rips open the biggest one first. Louise gives Rachel a gift.

> MARIA
> Slow down Rebecca, you might break it.

> LOUISE
> For you.

Rachel opens it: a manuscript of "Flowers and Friends."

> RACHEL
> "To Rachel, who never stopped until she got it right."

> LOUISE
> What with all you've gone through, I stopped feeling sorry for myself and finished my book.

> MARIA
> (sarcastic)
> Congratulations.

> SAM
> Now she'll have time to darn my socks.

They all laugh.

> LOUISE
> You wish.

Rebecca opens her present: a painting of a seashore.

> RACHEL
> (to Rebecca)
> I thought you would want it; your mother painted it for me a few years ago.

Rebecca runs out of the room. Rachel goes after her.

Rebecca's BEDROOM:

Rebecca gets under her covers.

> RACHEL (cont'd)
> Your mother was a wonderful artist.

No answer. Rachel waits, starts to exit.

> REBECCA
> You going to die too?

INT. SILVER SPRINGS HOME - NIGHT

Louise types while Rachel dictates. Maria thumbs through Rachel's manuscript while she watches t.v.

> RACHEL (DICTATING)
> DDT, short for dichloro-diphenyl-trichloro-ethane - a chlorinated hydrocarbon.

> LOUISE
> Poetry, pure poetry.

Maria reads Rachel's writing:

> MARIA
> Some organic compounds are simply combinations of carbon and hydrogen. The simplest of these is methane.

> LOUISE
> Chemistry is definitely not my forte.

                    MARIA
          You and the rest of us.

                    RACHEL
          I sent Bill a few chapters.

                    LOUISE
          And?

                    RACHEL
          Haven't heard yet.

Rachel gets up to look at Maria's painting. Maria covers the painting so Rachel can't see it.

                    MARIA
          Wait 'til it's finished.

INT. SILVER SPRINGS HOME - SPRING - NIGHT

RACHEL'S BEDROOM: Rachel's POV as she writes in bed: it's raining hard outside the bedroom window. She's weary. She reads a letter.

                    LOUISE (V.O.)
          Sam is concerned that Dr. Manfred will be
          disqualified because his German education
          is in medicine, not chemistry. But Mr.
          Bedford the beekeeper-

She rubs her eyes. The letter appears blurred. With difficulty, she continues reading.

> RACHEL
> – Mr. Bedford is quite a credible witness…Rachel, this is Sam, thanks for writing Dr. Lehman, he'll give 'em hell. Haven't heard from crazy Eliot, only our single most important witness. We're counting on you to…

She can't make out what it says. She rests for a second, rubs her eyes. She gets up, gingerly, walks to her dressing table. She rubs her temples, looks at herself in the mirror.

She lowers her pajama top to

EXPOSE HER BREASTS: nothing left but scar tissue. She looks noble.

INT. BOSTON COURTROOM - DAY

Susan HINDS, attorney for Mrs. Spock, Sam, and Louise (at the plaintiff's table). She questions DR. CHARLES MANFRED, a thin German, stained tie. In the gallery, Rachel takes notes, Rebecca sharpens a pencil for her. At the opposition's desk, STANLEY TURNER, grey pinstripe suit lawyer, and BLACK-ROBERTS. On the bench, JUDGE WALTER BRUCHHAUSEN, covertly playing a word puzzle.

> DR. MANFRED
> As far as what effect DDT has on the soil, the results are inconclusive.

Black-Roberts watches Rachel, shuffling through her notes, wearing dark glasses. She hands Rebecca a note card which she hands to Louise who gives it to Hinds. She reads it, then:

> HINDS
> And on plants?

DR. MANFRED
Well, we've discovered that the residue
is as high, or higher in some cases, than
when originally sprayed.

HINDS
Higher than the initial application?

Rachel starts coughing. Rebecca looks worried:

DR. MANFRED
Interesting, don't you think? We think
the plants absorb the additional DDT from
the water supply.

HINDS
Thank you, sir.

Mrs. Spock congratulates Hinds on her scoring tactic. Black-Roberts confers with Turner.

TURNER
Dr. Manfred, where were you educated sir?

DR. MANFRED
Switzerland.

TURNER
But you are German.

DR. MANFRED
Now, I am American.

TURNER
Good for you. Correct me if I am wrong,
but weren't you forced to leave the
University in Munich because of your
radical ideas on soil conservation!

Rachel starts coughing again. Black-Roberts pours a glass of water, and with a curious smile hands it to Rachel.

>   HINDS
> Objection, the witness is not here for
> character assassination.

                              CUT TO:

On the witness stand, DR. PHILIP HARLOWE, waxed mustache. Rebecca is busy assembling a COOTIE (plastic insect); Rachel passes a note to Rebecca, who hands it to LOUISE, who hands it to Hinds, who reads it.

>   HINDS
> Has there, then, been, since the
> introduction of DDT, an increase in
> environmental diseases suffered by
> workers in the agriculture industry?

>   DR. HARLOWE
> A remarkable increase: since 1950, eighty
> five percent higher incidence. Field
> workers complain of skin cancers, and
> there's been an alarming increase in
> birth defects in families who work in
> cotton fields.

>   HINDS
> What about ordinary folk like myself, who
> use pesticides in the home?

Rachel's vision starts to blur; she SEES WHITE SPOTS:

          DR. HARLOWE
In the general populace, we've seen a
thirteen percent increase in lymphomas, a
twenty five percent increase in leukemia.

          HINDS
Thank you, Dr. Harlowe.

Rachel is queasy. Black-Roberts hands Turner a note.

Louise realizes Rachel is very sick. She quietly goes to
Rachel. (While they talk, in the b.g. Turner questions Dr. Harlowe:
Turner: "Dr. Harlowe, are you aware that it is official
government policy to accept some medical risks associated
with nuclear testing and fallout?"
Dr. Harlowe: "Yes, I am aware of that unfortunate policy, but
it doesn't give chemical companies the right to expose the
public to possible genetic defects and cancer.")

          LOUISE
You okay?

          RACHEL
Sorry.

          LOUISE
It doesn't look too good.

          RACHEL
Eliot will set things straight.

          LOUISE
If he ever shows up.

Rachel FAINTS.

INT. HOSPITAL - NIGHT

On the hospital t.v.: the ED MURROW show: JACKIE KENNEDY shows off the WHITE HOUSE. Louise, with Rebecca asleep in her lap, and Sam wait in the hall. Rachel receives intravenous fluids. DR. PHILIP ROBERTS, pince-nez glasses:

>RACHEL
>But–

>DOCTOR ROBERTS
>– No ifs, ands, or buts. Rest, rest, and more rest. I only wish I could go with you. Maine is delightful this time of year.

He exits. Eliot knocks, enters. He is drunk.

>RACHEL
>Well, if it isn't my knight in shin...

She coughs, can't talk. He gives her water, pours himself a drink from his silver flask. They clink glasses.

>ELIOT
>I heard a good one the other day. Know why Nixon lost the election??? Even his dog Checkers is a card-carrying Democrat. Scuttlebutt is that if I testify, I get the steel boot instead of the gold watch.

>RACHEL
>They can't fire you for telling the truth.

> ELIOT
> Can't they?

> NURSE
> I'm sorry sir, no visitors.

> ELIOT
> I'd ask you to dance, but...

She manages a smile; he exits. At the door, Sam:

> SAM
> (to Eliot)
> You plan on testifying tomorrow?

> ELIOT
> What's the point?

INT. U.S. DISTRICT COURTROOM, BOSTON - DAY

Mrs. Spock and Sam sit at the plaintiff's table. Eliot is drunk.

> HINDS
> Can you describe, factually, what exactly chlordane does to the body?

> ELIOT
> Factually? It kills you, penetrates the skin. In point of fact, anyone handling it could be poisoned. More to the point, it is so damn toxic to the liver and kidneys that- did I mention it's four to five times more poisonous than the old bugaboo- DDT?

> HINDS
> And what percentage of our food supply do you suppose has chlordane in it?

> ELIOT
> Percentage? I dunno. The sad truth is that these bastards don't know either.

> JUDGE
> Dr. Stanford!

> ELIOT
> Sorry your honor. These gentlemen, in a polite way, make sure chlordane, DDT, and a thousand other chemicals are used in the production of most American grain, fruit, vegetables. And an even sadder fact, pathetic fact actually, is not one of them know the amount of residue in the...in the...I forgot what I was saying.

> HINDS
> No one has yet to determine how much chlordane or DDT or whatever toxin is in the food we eat day in, day out?

> ELIOT
> Bingo. I've tried to get a program underway, but...

Louise and Rebecca with Rachel, weak, enters. Rachel gives an encouraging smile to Eliot.

> HINDS
> Thank you sir. Your witness.

TURNER
Dr. Stanford, you work for the Dept. of Agriculture, is that right?

ELIOT
Last time I checked, yes.

TURNER
Then, you must be aware that your own agency has conducted study after study and unequivocally guarantees the safety of our food supply.

ELIOT
A pack of lies if ever–

TURNER
And are you aware that similar corroborating studies have been conducted at other universities?

ELIOT
Most of those studies you're talking about were bought and paid for by these same monkeys who pay your salary.

TURNER
Your honor, please.

JUDGE
Answer the question only sir.

TURNER
To refresh your memory, let me quote a study done by your own colleagues: "We believe chlordane to be the safest of all available organic insecticides."

ELIOT
They're all idiots! Chlordane is four times more dangerous–

TURNER
– But they based their conclusions, in part, on your very own statistics.

Turner hands Eliot the study. Eliot's POV: Rachel can't hide her disappointment in Eliot.

ELIOT
Let me see that. I didn't write this, and even if I did, you'd have to be a munchkin in Oz not to realize chlordane is a radical carcinogen!

TURNER
But you know, as well as Dr. Black-Roberts here...

INT. TRAIN STATION - BAR - NIGHT

Rachel, Rebecca, Sam, Mrs. Spock, Louise, and Eliot commiserate at the bar.

MRS. SPOCK
How long did it take the Judge to rule- two hours?

ELIOT
(downing another drink)
It's a good thing we don't drink.

SAM
We'll get them on appeal.

LOUISE
If our money holds out.

ELIOT
It won't.

MRS. SPOCK
Here's to life.

REBECCA
And the hereafter.

RACHEL
(to Mrs. Spock)
Thank you for all you've done.

MRS. SPOCK
We'll have to wait for your book to come out and see if that doesn't give them a swift kick in the you know what.

ELIOT
No, Mrs. Spock– what?

MRS. SPOCK
Well, we don't want to miss our train. Say goodbye Miss Polly.

MISS POLLY
Good bye Miss Polly.

Everyone laughs at Miss Polly's attempt at humor.

ALL
Goodbye, good luck.

Mrs. Spock and Miss Polly exit. They pass Black-Roberts, who enters the bar.

BLACK-ROBERTS
Well, this is a surprise.

ELIOT
Ah our savior.

BLACK-ROBERTS
Allow me to buy you and your friends a drink, to show there are no hard feelings.

RACHEL
Really, it's not–

BLACK-ROBERTS
– Nonsense, I insist. Waiter, another round if you please.

SAM
Tell me Doctor, how do you stand to look at yourself in the mirror?

LOUISE
Pardon my husband, he's taken a vow of honesty.

RACHEL
Please, all of you.

BLACK-ROBERTS
Don't think I take it at all personally, Miss Carson. Galileo, Pasteur, they all endured similar misinformed ridicule.

RACHEL
And if you're wrong?

BLACK-ROBERTS
As a Harvard trained chemist, let me ease your fears, good lady. I do not know, nor have I ever heard of one single case of ill health due to approved chemicals.

ELIOT
You must be dumb & deaf then.

RACHEL
But I have studied several cases that contradict your claims of safety.

BLACK-ROBERTS
You can't mean all those bogus cancer predictions. You're familiar with the imminent professor of Public Health at Harvard, Dr. Frederick Stare.

LOUISE
Waiter, do you have any aspirin?

The LOUD SPEAKER announces trains to the North.

BLACK-ROBERTS
He not only invalidates your unfortunate and alarmist point of view, but categorically states that we have the strictest environmental controls in history.

ELIOT
I'll drink to that.

                    SAM
          Excuse us, but we've a train to catch.

                    BLACK-ROBERTS
          Always a pleasure. Miss Carson,
          good luck with your little book.

INT. F.B.I. HEADQUARTERS – DAY

J. EDGAR HOOVER, on the phone, at his desk.

                    HOOVER
          But you've won the court case... A book?

KNOCK on door.

                    HOOVER (cont'd)
          Enter. Just a second.

PABLO GARCIA, a beautiful young Cuban, enters, hands Hoover a folder.

                    HOOVER (cont'd)
          Thank you, Pablo. Okay, I have the
          file. Don't worry, yes. Goodbye.

Pablo fixes them both a drink while Hoover opens the folder and flips through pictures of Rachel, Eliot, Sam, Louise. Hoover is particularly interested in a picture of Rachel holding hands with Louise, walking along a beach.

EXT. RACHEL CARSON'S MAINE COTTAGE – DAY

Rachel writes, Maria paints, Rebecca plays. She notices a car coming, runs to it. Ellen and Bill drive up.

RACHEL
Ellen, Bill, how good to see you.

BILL
You're looking chipper, like your old self.

RACHEL
Miracle of modern chemistry!

REBECCA
Did you bring me a surprise?

MARIA
Rebecca!

ELLEN
Let me see. A pen for Rachel.

Rebecca's disappointed.

RACHEL
How thoughtful.

ELLEN
And for Maria.

Ellen hands her an old oak frame. Rebecca is disappointed.

MARIA
It's too nice for my little picture.

ELLEN
Oh, I almost forgot.

She gives Rebecca a butterfly net.

                    RACHEL
          The monarchs didn't return this spring.

                    ELLEN
          No?

                    BILL
          Well, we still have the ocean- and the
          moon! Right, little lady?

He lifts Rebecca up on his shoulders, turns around and around as they all notice the full moon rising on the horizon.

                    MARIA
          That's right, they can't take that away-
          can they?

EXT. BEACH - NIGHT - FULL MOON

Ellen and Rebecca look for constellations through their telescope. Bill cooks over a fire pit. Rachel is tense.

                    RACHEL
          My potato salad's better than ever, if I
          do say so myself.

                    BILL
          Good, good, how's the chicken?

He hands a taste to Rachel.

                    RACHEL
          A little underdone. Well?

                    BILL
          Your book? A little overdone.
          The first chapter is brilliant, the
          description of the eagle, the deer in the

pine wood, as good as anything
you've written. After that, well Anne
read it, so did Eddie.

    RACHEL
And?

    BILL
I thought, maybe, once you're feeling–

    RACHEL
Please Bill.

    BILL
It's brilliant, technically, but it's so
dense with scientific data, reports,
figures, tables–

    RACHEL
– I thought accuracy was–

    BILL
– It's unreadable, Rachel. You've
forgotten who your readers are. Making a
damaging case against the government and
the chemical industries won't do much
good if nobody understands you.

Rachel is stunned.

    RACHEL
Rebecca, dinner's ready.

She takes the chicken up to the cottage.

BILL
Rachel.

INT. RACHEL'S COTTAGE - NIGHT

At the dinner table, stone silence.

MARIA
Louise and I both tried to warn you.
Even I had a hard time reading-

RACHEL
- Pass the salad.

BILL
Looks like the Russians are up to no good
in Cuba.

Rachel doesn't answer. She gets up, goes into her bedroom.

ELLEN
Rebecca, why don't we go out and see if
Orion has risen yet?

REBECCA
Okay.

They exit. Maria goes to Rachel's bedroom. The door is closed.

RACHEL'S BEDROOM:

Rachel reads her manuscript.

MARIA (V.O.)
Rachel?

Rachel doesn't answer. She throws down the manuscript.

>					MARIA (V.O.) (cont'd)
>			Rachel.

EXT. PINE WOODS - NIGHT

Mist falls through the pine woods as Rachel walks.

EXT. SEASHORE - DAY

Rebecca finds a small crab, shows it to Rachel, wrapped in a blanket and depressed. She smiles at Rebecca's find, but doesn't say anything. She walks away, dejected.

INT. RACHEL'S COTTAGE - NIGHT

RAIN, LIGHTNING, THUNDER. Unable to sleep, Rachel gets out of bed, turns on the light, finds her manuscript, and reads. She crosses out page after page.

INT. RACHEL'S COTTAGE - EARLY MORNING

Rachel is asleep at her desk. Rebecca enters with a record. She puts it on: Beethoven. Rebecca picks up Rachel's manuscript. Rachel wakes.

>					REBECCA
>			I can read- a little.

She holds her, tries to hold back her tears.

EXT./INT. RACHEL'S COTTAGE - DAY

Maria watches Rebecca fly a kite. Rachel enters with her manuscript.

> RACHEL
> Bill's right. Thickheaded, pretentious,
> I can't bear to read it.

Rachel goes to her desk on the SCREEN PORCH and types.

> RACHEL (cont'd)
> Simple, honest, sincere. And lots of
> footnotes at the end for ogres like Black-
> Roberts.

> MARIA
> Good. Good for you.

INT. RACHEL'S COTTAGE - NIGHT

Rachel takes her pills while she adds another page to a stack of pages. The moon is dazzling, throwing light across her desk. She doesn't notice. Rebecca enters, curls up on the divan, and goes to sleep.

INT. RACHEL'S COTTAGE - SUNRISE

A large stack of typed pages now, as Rachel sleeps at her desk.

Maria WALKS! into the room.

She reads a page, caresses Rachel, wakes her. Rachel puts her hand on Maria's.

Maria exits, WALKING!

More awake now, Rachel realizes what just happened. She exits into

MARIA'S BEDROOM:

Maria is in bed.

>   RACHEL
>   Mamma?

She goes to Maria's bed, looks at her. She feels Maria's face, realizes Maria is dead.

EXT. PENNSYLVANIA FARMLAND – DAY

NO SOUND.

SNOW falls gently.

Bill gives the eulogy, but we don't hear anything while Rachel, Rebecca (holding tight to Rachel), Ida, Louise, Sam, Ellen, Eliot, Cheryl, et al. mourn over Maria's grave.

Rachel's POV: her FATHER'S headstone inscription: "never forget the splendor in the grass, the glory in a flower." Bill offers his condolences to Rachel, then so does Ida, then Ellen: SOUND FADES UP.

>   ELLEN
>   We'll come visit, soon.

>   ELIOT
>   Soon as I find a job, I'll write.

Louise bursts into tears. Rachel comforts her.

>   SAM
>   Maria would have liked the spring snow.

Rebecca offers her hand to Rachel.

                    REBECCA
          Look.

She points to a crocus in the snow.

INT. RACHEL CARSON'S CHILDHOOD HOUSE - PENNSYLVANIA - NIGHT

Rebecca sleeps on the sofa. Rachel looks at pictures of herself as a child, with her Father, Mother, etc. Louise pours tea.

                    RACHEL
          I remember years ago, driving at night
          near the North Carolina coast. For hours
          I followed the lights of a car ahead. As
          long as I could see the light in front of
          me, I knew my way was clear. Mother was
          that kind of light.

                    LOUISE
          You've Rebecca, your book- me.

                    RACHEL
          I'm tired, I'm sick. I can't...

INT. RACHEL'S MAINE COTTAGE - DAY

Rachel sits at her desk, pecks at the typewriter a little, then stops. She's obviously blocked. Her POV: Louise and Rebecca outside working in the garden. Rachel pecks at the typewriter again, stops, pulls the paper out, throws it away. Her hands hurt. She goes into

MARIA'S ROOM:

Everything as it was, including Maria's last painting, covered up, on the easel. She starts to take off the cloth cover, but stops when the telephone RINGS. She answers it.

> BILL (V.O.)
> Hello Rachel.

> RACHEL
> Bill, how are you?

> BILL (V.O.)
> Fine, fine. Busy. Listen, Ellen and I thought we might come up, boil up a few lobsters, maybe sneak a look at your rewrite.

In the b.g. the roar of BIPLANES approaching.

> RACHEL
> I don't have anything.

> BILL (V.O.)
> Oh.

> RACHEL
> I'm sorry.

> BILL (V.O.)
> Look, you take all the time you need.

The Biplanes are LOUDER. Rachel hears them, looks outside. Louise notices them too.

> RACHEL
> Thank you Bill.

>   BILL (V.O.)
> Rachel, you know, you could give it up,
> go back to your children's book, what was
> that delightful title?

>   RACHEL
> We'll see, Bill. My best to Ellen.

She calls from the window.

>   RACHEL
> Why don't you two please come in for a
> while?

>   LOUISE
> I could use a glass of lemonade.

>   REBECCA
> Me too.

They come inside; as Rachel closes the window, pulls down the shades, her POV: the Biplanes release clouds of DDT as they fly toward the house.

INT. RACHEL'S COTTAGE - NIGHT

Louise and Rebecca play Monopoly. Rachel reads through her manuscript, tearing up page after page.

>   LOUISE
> It'll come. Remember, I stared at blank
> pages day after day, night after night.

>   RACHEL
> I'm not going to write this book, I
> realize that now.

                    LOUISE GOODMAN
          Of course you will. You are your worst
          critic. With time, you'll-

                    RACHEL
          - I don't have more time, you understand
          me?

INT. RACHEL'S COTTAGE - DAY

Louise looks at Rachel sulking at her desk. Louise dials the
phone, closes the door so Rachel can't hear her.

                    LOUISE
          Hello. Fine, I suppose. You sober?

INT. RACHEL'S COTTAGE - DAY

Louise brings in a breakfast tray, but Rachel doesn't stir;
she fakes sleep. Rebecca peeks in.

                    LOUISE
            (to Rebecca)
          What say you and I go look for brown
          eagles near the ridge?

                    REBECCA
          Okay.

They exit. Rachel gets up. She has a hard time walking,
tries to stretch- everything aches. A KNOCK on her bedroom
door. She doesn't answer it.

                    ELIOT (O.S.)
          Rachel? You can't fool an old government
          man, I know you're in there.

RACHEL
Go away.

He enters.

ELIOT
The last time you told me to go away, I didn't see you for how many years? (Beat) You hear about the DDT fiasco last week in Vermont?

RACHEL
What are you doing here?

ELIOT
I'm the new man in the Maine Dept. of Agriculture. And I've come to show you a few things, Rachel Louise Carson.

RACHEL
I can't.

ELIOT
If anybody can stop these fools, it's you. Rebecca, you ready?

Louise enters.

LOUISE
She will be in a minute.

RACHEL
I thought you two went off looking for eagles.

>   LOUISE
> Haven't been any eagles around these
> parts since they started spraying.

Rebecca enters with a small suitcase.

>   REBECCA
> Ready.

>   RACHEL
> I'm sorry, I can't, I'm sorry.

She closes the door on them.

INT. RACHEL'S COTTAGE - DAY

Rachel, in bed, watches the wind blow the leaves off the trees. A KNOCK on outside door.

>   RACHEL
> Rebecca? Louise?

KNOCK.

>   RACHEL
> Will someone get that?

KNOCK. She reluctantly gets up, and answers the door.

Two nondescript FBI MEN in trenchcoats.

>   FBI MAN
> Rachel Carson?

>   RACHEL
> Yes? Rebecca, is Rebecca all right?

> FBI MAN
> I wouldn't know ma'am.

Rachel's POV: Outside, Rebecca and Louise pick blueberries.

> RACHEL
> Who are you?

> FBI MAN
> F.B.I. We'd like to ask you a few questions, about certain inquiries–

> RACHEL
> – Inquiries, what are you talking about?

> FBI MAN
> Is it true, ma'am, that you were once a member of the Communist party?

> RACHEL
> Don't be ridiculous.

> FBI MAN
> We'd like to go over a few things regarding the adoption papers on one Rebecca–

> RACHEL
> Rebecca's my niece, I am in the process of legally adopting–

> FBI MAN
> May we come in?

Rachel pauses. She looks at Rebecca picking berries with Louise.

> RACHEL
> Do you have a warrant?

> FBI MAN
> Is it true you correspond with a Dr. Yanaslov Mayakofsky—

> RACHEL
> — Am I under arrest?

> FBI MAN
> No, but it—

> RACHEL
> Then you are trespassing, sir. Goodbye!

She slams the door. She is outraged. She looks out the open window, sees the FBI Men approach Rebecca and Louise.

> RACHEL (cont'd)
> Rebecca! Louise! Come in the house, will you?

The Men stop. Rebecca and Louise walk briskly toward Rachel. The Men back off. Rachel goes into her

BEDROOM:

and packs. Rebecca and Louise enter.

RACHEL (cont'd)
No illness, or mama's death– she lived
eighty seven years, God bless her– or Dr.
Black-Roberts, even if his mother was a
suffragette, and certainly not the F.B.I.
is going to stop me from the work I have
to do.
(to Louise)
Will you please call Eliot and tell him
to get over here as soon as possible? And
Rebecca, you pack a lot of paints and
things to keep you busy. We've got work
to do.

LOUISE	REBECCA
Hallelujah!	Hooray!

EXT. FARM – UPSTATE VERMONT – DAY

Rachel and Eliot up front in a hay wagon, with a FARMER, while Louise and Rebecca ride in back. They slowly pass a field covered with a white powder, DIELDRIN. Hundreds of CATTLE dead or dying while GOVERNMENT WORKERS load the carcasses into trucks.

ELIOT
Dieldrin?

The Farmer sadly nods "yes."

INT. MOVING CAR – DAY

Louise reads in backseat. Rebecca, with binoculars, peers out the window. Eliot drives; Kennedy speaks on the radio about the Cuban Missile Crisis. Rachel looks ill.

          ELIOT
Kennedy's pushing that bald headed fat Bolshevik a little far, what do you think?

          RACHEL
Would you mind pulling over for just a minute?

Eliot stops. Rachel gets out and vomits. Louise pours her tea from a thermos, hands it to Rachel.

          REBECCA
Look, a red-winged black bird; see it Auntie Rachel? There, there!

          RACHEL
Yes, I see it, how beautiful.

          ELIOT
What do you say we call it a day?

          RACHEL
It's early and we've got work to do.

EXT. MOVING CAR – LOVE CANAL HOUSING PROJECT – DAY

They drive very slowly through a middle class Housing Project (Love Canal). Some houses are already fenced off. Signs posted: "DANGER: CHEMICAL CONTAMINATION." WORKMEN board up houses. Moving vans clutter the streets. A BOY, on crutches, with one leg, tries to carry his bat and glove to a moving van, but he drops it. His MOTHER tries to help him, but he won't let her.

INT. AIRPORT HANGAR – NIGHT

Rachel and Eliot stand in back of the crowded hangar. Several banners on the wall, placards held by PROTESTERS with slogans like "Stop the Spraying," "Dept. of Agriculture a MURDERER," "Silent Death," etc. Several PLAIN-CLOTHED FBI AGENTS, including the two FBI MEN who came to Rachel's house, mill about.

Robert Black-Roberts tries to speak over the shouting of hundreds of outraged CITIZENS.

> BLACK-ROBERTS
> Of course, those spray rig operators and pilots who are now unfortunately incapacitated are at fault–

> PROTESTERS
> – How many more you going to make sick? Stop the spraying!

> CROWD
> Stop now! Stop now!

BLACK-ROBERTS
I can assure you we have corrected any oversights and can now guarantee no industrial injuries if instructions-

PROTESTERS
- Greed kills. No more chemicals!

Black-Roberts signals the FBI Agents: one FBI AGENT hits a MAN carrying a sign, another FBI AGENT pushes a WOMAN chanting slogans, etc. A riot develops.

CROWD
Greed kills! Greed kills!

Eliot helps Rachel outside to safety.

EXT. MARY'S COTTAGE/BIRD SANCTUARY - DAY

Rebecca skips rocks on the lagoon while Louise and Sam show Rachel a falcon's nest with several broken eggs. In the b.g. Eliot smokes a cigarette, disgusted by the dying birds.

ELIOT
God damn idiots- excuse my French.

LOUISE
When the mother falcon nests, the eggs crack.

RACHEL
DDT inhibits the development of the shell membrane

LOUISE
- What the hell do they think it's doing to humans! Fuck the chemical companies- excuse my plain English.

EXT. DEPT. OF AGRICULTURE OCEAN FIELD STATION – DAY

In b.g. Eliot helps Rebecca climb a tree. They are inundated by a haze of mosquitoes. Rachel and Louise listen to a Dept. of Agriculture FIELD MAN.

> FIELD MAN
> Trouble is, after a few years of spraying, the mosquitoes became immune. Trouble now is, the DDT killed off all the mosquitoes' natural predators, and we got ten times more of the bloodsuckers than when we started.

A boat approaches with a spray rig.

> RACHEL
> Rebecca!

Eliot takes Rebecca back to the car.

> FIELD MAN
> Damn skeeters!

> LOUISE
> Thanks for your time.

They get back in the car. In the b.g. the spray rig boat sprays the pond as Eliot drives off.

INT. RACHEL'S MAINE COTTAGE – NIGHT

Rachel types late into the night. Louise reads while she pats Rebecca to sleep on the couch. Eliot corrects Rachel's pages.

>   LOUISE
> Sam is coming up tomorrow.

Rachel and Eliot too busy to respond.

>   LOUISE (cont'd)
> Just in case you two might want
> to take a little break, and, you know,
> live it up a little. Hello? Anybody
> home?

Rachel and Eliot still too busy to respond.

INT. RACHEL'S MAINE COTTAGE – DAY

Louise files notes while Rachel types. Rebecca brings Rachel a glass of tea. Eliot is asleep with Rachel's typewritten pages covering his face. Sam drives up, honks.

>   SAM
> Fine day for sailing.

>   REBECCA
> Yea!

Louise hands Rebecca a hat. She picks up a picnic basket, wine, etc. Rebecca finds her binoculars, puts them around her neck.

>   LOUISE
> Okay, we've got the food, Rebecca's
> binocs. Plenty of wine.

                    SAM
          Let's go.

                    LOUISE
          Rachel?

                    RACHEL
          You all go ahead, have a nice time.

                    LOUISE
          Nonsense, it's a beautiful day.

                    REBECCA
          I'm not going either.

                    RACHEL
          I want you to go.

                    REBECCA
          Not if you're not going.

She takes off his hat, puts her binocs down. She nudges Eliot awake.

                    REBECCA (cont'd)
          Time to get back to work, Uncle Eliot.

INT. RACHEL'S COTTAGE - NIGHT

Eliot reads the nearly completed book. Rebecca watches t.v.: "Ho!Ho!Ho!" JOLLY GREEN GIANT commercial. Rachel sets the dinner table. She looks at Eliot to get a rise, but he just turns another page.

                    RACHEL
          Rebecca, come help set the table.

INT. RACHEL'S COTTAGE - LATER

Everyone sits around the table eating soup. Eliot reads the manuscript while he eats his soup.

>LOUISE
>You going back to Maryland this fall?

>RACHEL
>Rebecca has to go to school.

>SAM
>The piece de resistance!

Sam enters with a beautiful roast and all the trimmings.

>LOUISE
>You've really outdone yourself Sam.

>SAM
>No applause necessary.

>RACHEL
>Bravo Sam.

>SAM
>A jack of all trades.

>LOUISE
>And master of one or two I can think of.

She kisses him.

>SAM
>Rare or medium, Eliot? Eliot?

Eliot is too busy writing notes on Rachel's manuscript.

INT. RACHEL'S COTTAGE - LATE NIGHT

Rachel reads in bed. Her eyes hurt. A KNOCK on her door. She puts on her glasses, straightens up her bathrobe.

> ELIOT
> You decent?

> RACHEL
> Come in, Eliot.

He enters with her manuscript full of paper flags throughout. He pours himself a drink, drinks it down.

> RACHEL (cont'd)
> That bad, huh?

> ELIOT
> I don't know how to tell you this.

> RACHEL
> You hate it, it's stupid propaganda-

> ELIOT
> No-

> RACHEL
> - Maybe I've misinterpreted the danger, somehow I've-

> ELIOT
> - Will you stop? You have expressed everything I've ever wanted to say on the subject. The writing is superb- informed, intelligent, and what's really surprising, it's easy to read.

RACHEL
You're humoring me. You hate it, really. You're just trying to protect me because of my–

ELIOT
– If you'd pipe down for a second, you'd realize I'm trying to compliment you. Particularly on Chapters 1-7, some of the finest writing I've ever read.
   (Beat)

RACHEL
However.

ELIOT
However, the section on aerial spraying– Why give the chemical boys a break? Go after them with a vengeance. For example, on the subject of misappropriation of government funds for research on chemical drift–

RACHEL
– You really like it?

ELIOT
You still have some work to do. Wait until you see my notes. You sure you checked how many states are involved in the DDT fire ant eradication?

She hugs him.

RACHEL
Thank you Eliot, thank you.

EXT./INT. RACHEL'S COTTAGE – MORNING

ON THE PORCH:

Rachel types furiously.

IN THE GARDEN:

Rebecca shows Louise her painting.

> LOUISE
> She's good, very good.

> RACHEL
> She's got the Carson gift.

ON THE PORCH:

Rachel types the last word, takes the paper out of the typewriter, puts it with the final manuscript, turns the folder cover to the beginning. We see the title *Silent Spring*.

She exits to GARDEN:

> RACHEL (cont'd)
> Done, finally, absolutely, mercifully done!

Louise throws her arms around her. They dance, Rachel laughs and laughs. Louise laughs!

> LOUISE
> (to Rebecca)
> Come dance.

REBECCA
There's no music.

RACHEL
Listen.

They hear the WIND and they DANCE.

EXT./INT. RACHEL'S COTTAGE - DAY

IN THE GARDEN:

Rebecca and Rachel pick daises.

REBECCA
I miss the butterflies.

RACHEL
Me too.

Phone RINGS. She goes inside to the

PORCH:

and answers the phone:

RACHEL (cont'd)
Hello. Bill? Sitting down? Okay.
I'm a big girl, don't be silly.

She listens. As Bill talks, Rachel sits down. While she talks, her POV: CANADIAN GEESE MIGRATING.

> RACHEL (cont'd)
> You mean it Bill? You're not just...Come now, it's not that good...thank you, thank you...Yes, I thought there may be some legal problems... No, I won't worry, that's your job. Okay, yes, goodbye.

She hangs up, goes to the window to watch the geese honking their way across the early morning sky.

> RACHEL (cont'd)
> Rebecca, look.

She starts to exit, but suddenly her knees buckle. She falls. She tries to get up, but can't. She hears Rebecca coming. With great difficulty, she pulls herself up before Rebecca comes in.

> RACHEL (cont'd)
> Look darling!

She hands Rebecca her binoculars, and she looks at the geese.

> RACHEL (cont'd)
> Now that I've finished my book, we can go back to Maryland for a while.

> REBECCA
> You said we could stay here all summer.

> RACHEL
> We have so much to do.

Rebecca hugs her.

                REBECCA
        You're sick again, huh?

She holds her tight, tries to hold back her tears.

INT. HOSPITAL - WASHINGTON D.C. - RADIATION ROOM -DAY

Dr. Rogers places Rachel in the correct position.

                DR. ROGERS
        If you had rested like you promised, we
        might not be here today.

He signals the Nurse Technician to start, then exits. Rachel closes her eyes as the radiation machine starts.

INT. RACHEL'S SILVER SPRINGS, MARYLAND HOME - NIGHT

Louise helps Rebecca with her math; Rachel reads while lying down. Phone RINGS.

                LOUISE
        Don't you cheat now.

Louise ANSWERS the phone.

                LOUISE (cont'd)
        Hello Bill. Rachel? She ran off with a
        handsome...of course she's here. It's
        Bill, and he's grouchy.

She gives the phone to Rachel, goes back to Rebecca.

             RACHEL
Hello. I'm... I'm the same. ...to
Boston?...I don't...*The New Yorker?* How
wonderful.
       (to Rebecca and Louise)
The New Yorker is going to publish three
chapters of *Silent Spring* before the book
comes out.

             REBECCA
Goody, we'll be rich.

             RACHEL
Yes...yes...but we expected problems with
the chemical companies... Out of the
question...I'm exhausted, that's why.
Black-Roberts? An injunction?

INT. MOVING TRAIN - DAY

Rebecca's POV through her binoculars: a PEANUTS CARTOON (about Rachel saving the world) that a MAN at the other end of the rail car is reading. Louise and Rachel read through press clippings.

A COLLEGE COED reads *The New Yorker*, the sub-cover featuring Silent Spring. Rachel's POV: a BUSINESSMAN also reading *The New Yorker* article, a WOMAN feeding her BABY with a bottle also reading it, etc. Rachel hands Louise a press clipping.

             RACHEL
According to this I am an hysterical
spinster who hates children.

             LOUISE
That's a McCarthyism.

> RACHEL
> Meaning?

> LOUISE
> Nothing much, just that you're probably a communist or at the very least – a good looking lesbian.

She reads from the Chemical and Engineering News.

> RACHEL
> Miss Carson's attack on the New Jersey pest control management project is a frivolous attempt to give weight to all those nature-balancing, organic gardening, bird-loving unreasonable citizenry.

> LOUISE
> You'll survive: bird-loving isn't a crime, even in New Jersey.

INT. HOUGHTON MIFFLIN OFFICES – BOSTON – DAY

ELEVATOR:

Rachel is in her mother's wicker wheelchair. The elevator stops, Louise wheels her out.

> RACHEL
> Right here is fine.

Louise stops. She helps Rachel stand up. Rachel walks, with a cane, into the Houghton-Mifflin offices.

EDITORIAL OFFICES:

Rachel enters. Several SECRETARIES, OFFICE PERSONNEL, etc. rise, and CLAP for her. She is embarrassed.

INT. BILL'S OFFICE - DAY

Raymond Sadler, Bill, and Rachel at a table, with scores of letters, articles about Silent Spring.

> RAYMOND
> That kind of negative propaganda, in the chemical industry magazines, isn't a problem, legally that is.

> BILL
> In fact, it may gain us more attention than we could ever afford through advertising.

> RAYMOND
> But the threat of law suits by several chemical companies –

> RACHEL
> – Let them sue, everything in the book has been checked and re-checked.

> RAYMOND
> Good, but they can still sue for malicious–

> RACHEL
> – Malicious?

> RAYMOND
> Veliscol Chemical charges you've misrepresented the toxicity of chlordane and DDT.

RACHEL
I've only dealt with facts, period.

RAYMOND
At the very least they'll get an injunction to stop publication.

BILL
Unless we counter.

RAYMOND
It's the oldest defense in the world: attack the messenger.

BILL
And because the chemical companies have so damn much money–

RAYMOND
– They can and will stop publication of the book, unless we go after them.

RACHEL
You've my permission to do whatever.

RAYMOND
I don't think you understand. What we will require–

BILL
Rachel, we need you to launch the defense.

RAYMOND
We've already contacted President Kennedy's Secretary of the Interior–

BILL
– Stuart Udall, and he's sympathetic, but he needs us to get the ball...

RACHEL
I'm sorry Bill, but I wouldn't know how to even begin fighting–

RAYMOND
– C.B.S. Reports–

BILL
– They want to do a special on television, an exposé on pesticides–

RAYMOND
– Millions of people will be watching. If the public is behind you, Miss Carson, the chemical companies might just back down.

RACHEL
If I understand you correctly, you want me to go on national television!

BILL
And defend your book.

RACHEL
Defend against whom?

BILL
Robert Black-Roberts will speak for the Chemical Industry.

RACHEL
I'm sorry, I'm not, I'm sick, tired, I can't.

> RAYMOND
> Think it over Miss Carson. What about that chemist, Eliot Stanford, he could stand in for her.

> BILL
> Listen Rachel, you know I'll do everything humanly possible to get this book published, even if we do have to fight all the way to the Supreme Court.

> RAYMOND
> That'd tie it up, at the very least, three years.

> RACHEL
> Three years!

> RAYMOND
> Maybe even longer.

Bill realizes Rachel is devastated.

> BILL
> Raymond.

INT. HOTEL SUITE - NIGHT

BEDROOM: Rachel gives herself an injection.

FRONT ROOM: Rebecca and Louise play darts.

> LOUISE
> Bull's-eye.

> REBECCA
> Un't uh.

LOUISE
Well, almost.

RACHEL (O.S.)
Anyone want ice cream?

KNOCK on the door.

RACHEL (O.S.) (cont'd)
If that's Bill, I'm asleep.

Louise enters the

BEDROOM:

LOUISE
A reporter from *Time* magazine.

RACHEL
Tell him to come in.

SHEILA BARNES - chain-smoker in high heels, enters.

LOUISE
(sardonic)
I'd ask you in, but...

Louise exits.

RACHEL
Hello.

SHEILA
Sheila Barnes, *Time* magazine. Miss Carson, Time is running an article on your piece in *The New Yorker*.

RACHEL
I'm flattered.

SHEILA
Basically, our science editor has written that you "use emotion-fanning words," oversimplify, and that your book is down right, uh, misleading and inaccurate – at best.

RACHEL
Your editor is wrong. My position is clear and accurate, based on months of exhaustive research.

REBECCA AND LOUISE (O.S.)
Ice cream! Ice cream!

SHEILA
Then you refute our editor's claim that your analysis of pesticide contamination in America's drinking water is "unfair, one-sided, and hysterical?"

RACHEL
It doesn't take a science editor to understand that if you add DDT to a reservoir, you are threatening the purity of the drinking water. Good night, Miss Barnes.

SHEILA
How about your reaction–

Rebecca enters the bedroom.

                    REBECCA
– You promised we'd go get ice cream.

Louise enters.

                    LOUISE & REBECCA
Ice cream, ice cream, we all scream for
ice cream.

                    RACHEL
Miss Barnes was just leaving.

                    SHEILA
Yes, as a matter of fact. Good night.

INT. HOTEL ELEVATOR – NIGHT

Rachel in her mother's wicker wheelchair, Rebecca on her lap, Louise stands next to them.

                    REBECCA
We going to Maine soon, like you
promised?

The elevator door opens: a GANG of REPORTERS are waiting for Rachel.

                    REPORTER
Miss Carson, is it true the F.B.I. has
you under investigation for subversion?

                    RACHEL
Not that I am aware.

REPORTER #2
Care to comment on the statement by the
chief horticulturist at Michigan State
that your article "is more poisonous than
the pesticides you condemn?"

LOUISE
I hope he has job security.

REPORTER #3
Are you aware that Professor Frederick
Stare of Harvard claims your article is
propaganda and should simply be ignored?

RACHEL
Apparently it hasn't been.

REPORTER #4
Miss Carson, any truth to the
accusation that you have cancer and have
tried to blame your illness on
pesticides?

This one gets to her.

LOUISE
Excuse us, please!

REBECCA
Leave her alone.

REPORTER #5
Fifteen years ago, were you dismissed
from the Dept. of Fish and Wildlife
because of unprofessional conduct?

> REPORTER #6
> Miss Carson, why is it you never married?
> Is she your "companion?"

Louise manages to get the elevator doors closed.

> RACHEL
> We're going back to Maine.

> REBECCA
> Goody.

> LOUISE
> What about the t.v. show?

> RACHEL
> They'll have to get Eliot.

INT. RACHEL'S MAINE COTTAGE – NIGHT

Rachel's BEDROOM:

is strewn with letters. She reads one, frowns, opens another; it is written in cut-out letters, like a ransom note: "GO BACK TO RUSSIA WHERE YOU BELONG."

She goes into

Rebecca's BEDROOM.

She is asleep. Rachel goes into

MARIA'S BEDROOM:

She notices the covered PAINTING Maria was working on before she died. Rachel uncovers it. It is almost an exact rendering of Rachel's DREAM: Rachel and her Father walking under a starry sky. Under the painting is a title: "The Night They Heard the Heavenly Music."

PHONE RINGS. She stares at the painting while the PHONE RINGS RINGS RINGS.

INT. CBS STUDIOS - DAY

Eliot, very nervous, takes a drink from his flask, offers one to the MAKE-UP ARTIST. Black-Roberts, confident, sits across the table, facing ERIC SEVAREID.

        BLACK-ROBERTS
Too bad about Miss Carson.

        ELIOT
Asshole.

Various T.V. PERSONNEL milling about until the red light in t.v. camera goes on. The DIRECTOR signals Sevareid:

        ERIC SEVAREID
We are living in what has been called "The Synthetic Age"- the Age of the Atom, the Missile, the Frozen T.V. Dinner. Tonight we look at the modern dilemma of living in the Age of the Wormless Apple and the Calculated Risk. Our controversy begins with- the insect. Damage caused by pests, in this country alone–

FOOTAGE of FARMERS holding up pest-damaged crops; scenes in Africa where malaria-carrying mosquitos cause sickness and death; Veliscol Chemical's plant: DDT being manufactured:

> SEVAREID (V.O.)
> – is an estimated fourteen billion dollars a year. Today, man's defense rests primarily on chemical poisons. Brewed in flasks and test tubes–

Off t.v. camera, RACHEL ENTERS, accompanied by Sam, Louise, Rebecca. Black-Roberts is a little unnerved by Rachel's sudden entrance. Eliot helps her out of her wheelchair, then joins Rebecca, et al. off camera. The Makeup Artist quickly prepares Rachel, just in time before she speaks:

> SEVAREID (cont'd)
> – synthetic organic pesticides are the major weapon. However, since *The New Yorker* magazine published a selection from biologist Rachel Carson's yet unpublished book, *Silent Spring*, a national quarrel has begun. Miss Carson:

Rachel is nervous but becomes more confident as she speaks.

> RACHEL
> Since the early days of World War II, the government and the chemical industry have invented thousands of chemicals that we now use to kill insects, weeds, and whatever pest seems to bother us.

Footage of: 1. Biplanes spraying forests, 2. a HOUSEWIFE spraying her garden, etc.

> RACHEL (V.O.) (cont'd)
> Unfortunately, these toxic chemicals are
> poison; they leave harmful residues
> everywhere in our daily lives, deadly
> chemicals that we breathe, swallow, touch.
> Isn't it obvious that when such a deluge
> of chemicals surround and invade us that
> it may lead to terrible consequences,
> that to put it bluntly, that we are
> poisoning every man, woman, and child in
> America- indeed, throughout the entire
> planet.

Louise appears nervous. Rebecca claps for Rachel. Sam good naturedly stops her when the Assistant Director motions for Rebecca to quiet down.

> BLACK-ROBERTS
> My colleague and good friend, Miss
> Carson, unfortunately makes gross claims
> that are completely unsupported by
> scientific evidence. After all, she is a
> nature writer, not a chemist.

> RACHEL
> True, I am a "nature writer," but if you
> would condescend to at least read my
> book, Professor, you cannot avoid that
> all my "claims," as you call them, are
> supported by highly respected scientists-
> indeed, even by a few of your own Harvard
> colleagues.

BLACK-ROBERTS
But your suggestion that pesticides are in fact biocides, destroying all life, is absurd. The real threat, Miss Carson, to the survival of man is not chemical but biological, hordes of insects denuding our forests–

FOOTAGE of 1. Swarms of insects over a forest 2. Locusts attack a corn field 3. Famine in India.

BLACK-ROBERTS (V.O.) (cont'd)
– sweeping over crop lands, ravaging our food supply, leaving in their wake destitution and hunger.

RACHEL
Over the years that pesticides have been in use, insects have developed a resistance to the poisons we have used against them. We then began applying stronger concentrations of the pesticides, or the use of even more toxic, super poisons. The insects, over time, built up a resistance to these stronger remedies. We are now discovering that these deadly poisons cause leukemia, cancers of all sorts, and other terrible diseases.

BLACK-ROBERTS
Nonsense. Pesticides have contributed considerably to health in this country. Take, for example, the control of malaria. Back in 1935, we had over a hundred and fifty thousand cases of

malaria in the United States.
Today we have virtually none.

    RACHEL
Don't misunderstand me. I am not
advocating we must never use
insecticides. What we need to do is
insure that these poisons are used
properly, that we stop refusing to
acknowledge their potential for harm.

    BLACK-ROBERTS
Absolutely ridiculous.

    RACHEL
And that we have used these chemicals
willy-nilly, without any substantial
research as to their potential dangers to
humans, animals, to the planet itself.

    BLACK-ROBERTS
It is for the greater good that we
control nature and conquer these vermin
before they wipe us out.

    RACHEL
"The control of nature," dear professor,
is a rather difficult phrase. Your idea
of control has led to the development of
over 55,500 such control agents since
1945!

While Black-Roberts talks, Rachel coughs. Louise is alarmed.

    BLACK-ROBERTS
When pesticides are used in accordance
with instructions, there is no danger to
either man or wildlife.

                    RACHEL
    Really? Do you know to what extent the
    American populace is actually exposed?
    Did you know that less than one percent
    of the food supply is even tested for
    possible toxic residue?

INT. CBS TELEPHONE OPERATOR ROOM – SAME

The switchboard OPERATORS are overwhelmed by the number of incoming calls (switchboards lit up, etc.).

                    OPERATOR
    C.B.S. Miss Carson's book?

INT. CBS REPORTS STUDIO - SAME

                    BLACK-ROBERTS
    Miss Carson sends up a flag of
    unnecessary alarm. Most of these
    chemicals show only tiny residues that
    are of no real danger.

                    RACHEL
    Perhaps you are right. But are you sure,
    good sir, how often we ingest your
    chemical recipes? I argue it is the
    daily accumulation of these toxic poisons
    that potentially will end up giving all
    of us terrible diseases, even cause the
    death of untold numbers of innocent men,
    women, and children.

INT. CBS OPERATORS ROOM - SAME

The volume of calls has quadrupled.

> OPERATOR #2
> I don't know if your flea powder-

> OPERATOR #3
> - Chlordane? On your lawn?

INT. CBS REPORTS STUDIO - SAME

> RACHEL

We poison the dragon fly in America's wilderness, and the salmon runs begin to appear in fewer numbers, or when they do, they often have cancerous growths and ultimately die. Those that survive enter the food supply and we unknowingly ingest their disease. When we spray millions of natural preserves, the birds begin to die, scores of animal species disappear...

> BLACK-ROBERTS

- Once again, it's a trade off, the inevitable cost of progress. Would you have us overwhelmed by red ants, gypsy moths-

BEHIND THE CAMERAS:

> ELIOT
> - Progress my ass.

ON CAMERA:

> RACHEL
> But the human price, sir, why do you protest so little- -

> BLACK-ROBERTS
> - You are resorting to innuendo, exaggeration.

INT. HOUSE - CLEVELAND, OHIO -NIGHT

A typical American FAMILY - FATHER, BOY, GIRL - watching CBS REPORTS. In b.g. the MOTHER in the pantry, reading the labels on her insecticide.

> RACHEL (ON T.V.)
> Are you unaware of the sudden illnesses or even deaths of the men, women, and children who have been "accidentally" exposed-

EXT. N.Y.C. - BIG ED'S T.V. STORE - NIGHT

Hundreds of T.V.'s outside Big Ed's t.v. shop. A BUM drinks a bottle of milk while he watches Rachel.

> RACHEL (ON THE T.V. SCREENS)
> - Do you realize, Professor, that the young born today are exposed to your chemicals from the day of their birth, even in the breast milk when nursing-

The Bum looks at it, throws his bottle of milk away.

INT. CBS STUDIO - NIGHT

          RACHEL
What is going to happen to the children once they reach maturity? If we continue to apply the tens of thousands of tons of poison to our environment, are you ready to face the epidemic of cancers and disease that will cripple our great country by the 1980's? Is progress at any cost worth that legacy?

          BLACK-ROBERTS
I don't know, nor do you I might add.

BEHIND THE CAMERAS:

          ELIOT
She's got him now.

IN FRONT OF CAMERAS:

          RACHEL
It has been demonstrated, by your own colleagues, that these chemicals destroy the liver, the nervous system, producing unspeakable growth, mutations. Wouldn't you, a reasonable, intelligent man of science, at least suggest we put these chemicals under reasonable scrutiny?

          BLACK-ROBERTS
Once again, you make statements that are scientifically in error, calculated misinterpretation of facts.

> RACHEL
> Can you specifically–

She has a coughing spell.

> BLACK-ROBERTS
> – You deliberately depreciate all the safety measures which our researchers have laboriously developed–

> RACHEL
> – Forgive me sir, but I find it hard to fathom that you've laboriously developed safeguards for all fifty-five-thousand pesticides...

She can't continue because of her coughing.

> SEVAREID
> Thank you Dr. Black-Roberts and Miss Carson. We will return after these messages with a panel of scientists and Congressmen and continue our discussion.

OFF THE AIR sign lights up.

> DIRECTOR
> Eric, we've received over five thousand calls!

> SEVAREID
> Get Miss Carson a glass of water, will you please!

Rebecca runs to Rachel, but Sam stops her. Louise and Eliot go to help Rachel. She coughs so much she can't stop.

INT. HOUGHTON-MIFFLIN – SALES OFFICE – DAY

Bill, followed by several OFFICE BOYS carrying bags of mail, marches past OFFICE EMPLOYEES answering phones, taking orders for *Silent Spring*. He bursts into Raymond Sadler's office.

INT. HOUGHTON-MIFFLIN – RAYMOND SANDLER'S OFFICE – SAME

The Office Boys dump hundreds of letters on Raymond's desk.

          BILL
    Here's just today's mail– over ninety
    percent backing Rachel. That enough
    public support for you?

INT. HOSPITAL – DAY

Rachel lies in bed under an oxygen tent. Eliot enters, turns on the t.v.

          ELIOT
    There you are, lying flat on your back
    missing all the fun.

ON T.V.: PRESIDENT KENNEDY at White House Press Room. While the REPORTER asks Kennedy his question, J. EDGAR HOOVER enters with Pablo Garcia, his Assistant. Kennedy becomes self-conscious of Hoover's glare.

          REPORTER
    Mr. President, there appears to be a
    growing concern among scientists as to
    the possibility of dangerous long-term
    side effects from the use of DDT and
    other pesticides. Have you considered
    asking the Dept. of Agriculture or the
    Public Health Service to take a closer
    look at this?

As Kennedy answers, Hoover exits, angry.

> PRESIDENT KENNEDY
> Yes, and I know that they already are. I think particularly, of course, since Miss Carson's book, but they are examining the matter.

Eliot hands her a copy of *Silent Spring*.

> ELIOT
> Mind signing my copy? Could be worth a fortune someday.

She is too weak to hold the book.

INT. HOSPITAL – DAY

Louise combs through a stack of letters. Rachel is able to sit up now, looks better.

> LOUISE
> You'll love this one. "Every county farm agent in upstate New York has gone out of his way to assure his constituency that Miss Carson's book is nothing less than hysteria and nonsense. However, upon investigation, no one in either the country farm offices or at the state level had actually read the book, but to the man, all had disapproved of it heartily."

Enter Ellen, Bill, and Rebecca carrying a stuffed animal.

> REBECCA
> Auntie Rachel, look what I won at the circus.

ELLEN
Now don't worry; she only ate three hot
dogs, two cotton candies—

REBECCA
— And a bag of peanuts.

BILL
One of which I brought back for you as a
present in honor of the five-hundred
thousandth copy of *Silent Spring* sold, as
of last week. A hundred thousand more
copies go to press this week, and with
the Book of the Month club sales, I think
it's safe to say we will pass the million
copy figure by spring, when Houghton-Mifflin
will spare no expense to honor you with a
grand celebration.

REBECCA
We are going to Maine this spring, you
promised.

RACHEL
Sorry, Bill, but Rebecca's right. After
all, we have our children's book to
finish.

INT. RACHEL'S SILVER SPRING HOME – DAY

Louise helps Rachel dress (in her wicker wheelchair). A scarf
covers her head.

RACHEL
I must be mad, doing this the very day
we're leaving for Maine.

                    LOUISE
          You'd be crazy not to. Since when does a
          little itsy bitsy book have the power to
          change the political course of a nation?

Louise helps Rachel with her WIG.

                    RACHEL
          When the government gets involved, you
          can't be sure of anything.

INT. EXECUTIVE OFFICE HEARING ROOM – DAY

Room jammed with REPORTERS, T.V. CREWS, CONGRESSMEN, etc. taking pictures of Rachel, seated in her wheelchair, facing the President's Science Advisory Committee. DR. JEROME WIESNER, Kennedy's chief science advisor, speaks:

                    WIESNER
          Most of the public literature and the
          experiences of the President's Panel
          Members here indicate that, until
          publication of *Silent Spring* by Rachel
          Carson–

The Reporters, Guests (including Rebecca, Louise, Sam, Eliot), etc. break into a thunderous applause for Rachel. Dr. Wiesner uses his gavel to restore order.

                    WIESNER (cont'd)
          – until publication of Miss Carson's
          book, we were sadly unaware of the
          toxicity of pesticides. We therefore
          recommend that the President seek to
          establish an Environmental Protection
          Agency, and as their first duty, ban the
          chemical known as DDT due to its extreme
          danger–

Once again the crowd claps and yells their approval. Dr. Weisner speaks over the crowd's noise.

> WIESNER (cont'd)
> – and furthermore that it shall henceforth be the role of the government to regulate and inform the public of the hazards of pesticides. Miss Carson has kindly consented to give us a few moments of her time. Miss Carson.

Nervous, Rachel takes a drink.

> RACHEL
> Thank you Dr. Wiesner, members of the President's panel. I am pleased with much of your excellent report. However, the report alone does not–

EXT. RACHEL'S MAINE COTTAGE – DAY

Rachel, Bill, Eliot, Louise, Sam, Rebecca, and Ellen picnic in front of the cottage while watching Rachel on t.v. (perched on her desk facing outside) giving her speech in front of the President's Science Committee. Rachel looks through her new manuscript, *The Sense of Wonder*, with Sam's photos.

> RACHEL (ON T.V.)
> – solve the problem. It is important to remember that pressures, which opponents of reform know how to apply, will continue unabated. To that end, the decisions that will be made affect every individual. My only hope is that society will have the courage to do so.

Louise whispers to Rebecca who whispers something to Rachel. She nods yes. Louise and Rebecca wheel her down the path in her wicker wheelchair toward the pine woods.

EXT. PINE WOODS - DAY

Louise, Rebecca, and Rachel enter the pine woods:

> REBECCA
> Close your eyes.

Rachel closes her eyes. As they go further into the woods, monarch butterflies start flying about, first one, then another, then scores.

> LOUISE
> Okay, you can look now.

She opens her eyes. Her POV: Rebecca jumps and plays under thousands of MONARCH BUTTERFLIES. She is ecstatic, finally focusing on one solitary butterfly:

> RACHEL (V.O.)
> Most of all I will always think of the
> Monarchs, the way they eagerly follow one
> another, drawn together by a mystical
> power.

EXT. PINE WOODS - DAY

The CAMERA PANS down from the one BUTTERFLY to a funereal gathering of Eliot, Cheryl, Sam, Louise, Ida, Mrs. Spock, Miss Polly, Bill, Ellen, and Rebecca who allows the wind to blow Rachel's ashes out of an urn, out over the ocean.

                    RACHEL (V.O.) & REBECCA (V.O.)
          Each and every year, we watch for their
          return; happily some manage to find their
          way, some do not.

                    REBECCA (V.O.)
          For this is the way of all things, a
          natural cycle which we accept as the end,
          as it should and always will be.

CLOSE ON THE BUTTERFLY flying into RACHEL'S BLOWING ASHES.

FADE TO BLACK.

About the Author

Screenwriter, farmer, poet, critic, translator, film maker, director, producer, teacher — Paul Lobo Portugés is the author of *Saving, Grace, Hands Across the Earth, The Visionary Poetics of Allen Ginsberg, Aztec Birth, Paper Song, The Flower Vendor* and *The Body Electric Journal.* He has received awards from the Fulbright Commission, the Ford Foundation, the National Endowment, the UC Regents, the Focus Foundation, and the Briarcomb Foundation. At present, he is a Film & Media Studies Lecturer at the University of California, Santa Barbara.